To Harriet
Hope you will enjoy our cook book.
I understand you come to many of our
cooking schools. God Bless you.
Robert H. Mondavi
5-6-96

little Bacchus says

a day without wine
is a day
without sunshine
Margrit

/ MAY YOUR KITCHEN ALWAYS BE FILLED
WITH GOOD FRIENDS, FOOD, & WINE!
CAROLYN DILLE

Robert Mondavi,

Margrit Biever Mondavi,

and

Carolyn Dille

PHOTOGRAPHS BY

ROBERTO SONCIN GEROMETTA

MICHAEL SKOTT

SIMON METZ

ILLUSTRATIONS BY

MARGRIT BIEVER MONDAVI

DESIGN BY

BARBARA MARKS

Simon & Schuster

SEASONS
OF THE VINEYARD

CELEBRATIONS AND RECIPES FROM THE ROBERT MONDAVI WINERY

SIMON & SCHUSTER
Rockefeller Center
1230 Avenue of the Americas
New York, NY 10020

DESIGNED BY BARBARA MARKS

Manufactured in the United States of America

10 9 8 7 6 5 4 3 2 1

The recipes on pages 207 and 218 are from *Marcella Hazan's Italian Kitchen,*
by Marcella Hazan, copyright © 1986 by Marcella Polini Hazan and Victor Hazan,
reprinted by permission of Alfred A. Knopf, Inc.

Library of Congress Cataloging-in-Publication Data
Mondavi, Robert, date.
      Seasons of the vineyard: celebrations and recipes from the
Robert Mondavi Winery / Robert Mondavi, Margrit Biever Mondavi, and Carolyn Dille;
illustrations by Margrit Biever Mondavi; photographs by Roberto Soncin Gerometta,
Michael Skott, Simon Metz.
          p.   cm.
      Includes index.
      1. Cookery. 2. Menus. 3. Wine and wine making—California—Napa Valley.
4. Robert Mondavi Winery. I. Mondavi, Margrit Biever. II. Dille, Carolyn.
III. Robert Mondavi Winery. IV. Title.
TX714.M662 1996
641.5—dc20   96-4947
ISBN 0-684-80758-0

A leatherbound signed first edition of this book has been published by Easton Press.

The authors dedicate
this book to
Robert Mondavi's
mother,
Rosa Mondavi.

It was in her kitchen
Robert first learned
lifelong lessons about
food, cooking, and many
other wonderful basics
for the good life.

Acknowledgments

At the start: Linda Cunningham, Antonia Allegra, and, especially, Patricia Leasure.

At the winery: Mary Azevedo, Joan Dold, Axel Fabré, Nina Weymss, and, especially, Julie Prince.

In the kitchens and at the tables: Nancy Verde Barr, Michael Chipchase, Michel Cornu, Gary Jenanyan, Carol Mead, Marlee Rodrigue, Sarah Scott, and the Vineyard Room staff. Also, Forni-Brown Gardens, Calistoga; Karen Mitchell of Model Bakery, St. Helena; and The Napa Valley Olive Oil Manufacturing Company, St. Helena.

For assistance with props: Karen Frerichs, Calistoga Pottery, and Vanderbilt & Company, St. Helena.

For their special memories: Giulia Santi, Helen Ventura, Serena Ventura Chickering, and Ted Streshinsky for his early photographs of Robert and Rosa Mondavi.

For his perserverance: Roberto Soncin Gerometta.

From beginning to end: Harvey Posert, who made the first call, and Regina Lutz, both valuable beyond measure; Sydny Miner, our editor at Simon & Schuster, who helped our vision grow; and Martha Casselman, who cleared the path and kept everyone on it.

Contents

CELEBRATIONS AND RECIPES FROM THE ROBERT MONDAVI WINERY

Preface

Maybe because I'm a vintner, I love to eat. Starting with a full breakfast, I make sure I have three meals a day. My wife, Margrit, says, "Robert eats three *important* meals a day." However, I do not snack, and I exercise every day.

As a child in Lodi, on the northern edge of California's San Joaquin valley, I helped my mother, Rosa, get ready for the three hearty meals we had every day. I well remember her working the pasta dough and creating the agnolotti that was the main dish of many lunches. In those days, I never thought that food and wine would be so important for the rest of my life.

And not just my personal life. When I started the winery in 1966, we established our Vineyard Room to present our wines with compatible foods. As my family had entertained in the kitchen and dining room, so do we now for our friends in the wine trade, wine consumer groups, and others. Our To-Kalon—the best, or highest good, in Greek—vineyard surrounds the Vineyard Room where we taste special wines and cook special meals for our guests. To-Kalon was the name given to one of the earliest Napa Valley vineyards by pioneer winegrower Henry Crabb. We have been gratified that so many find food, wine, and the arts such a delightful experience in a vineyard setting.

Our cultural programs, always an integral part of our winery, have been given direction by Margrit. In 1969 we founded our Summer Music Festival of jazz and popular music to benefit the Napa Valley Symphony, and to complement the art exhibitions we were already sponsoring in the Vineyard Room Gallery. The festival has expanded to include the Classical Music Festival during the winter. In the 1970s we introduced the Great Chefs of France programs, now expanded to present the best chefs throughout the world in educational cooking programs at the winery. In all these programs, food, wine, and the arts complement each other as representations of a civilized life. We believe that music, painting and sculpture, drama and literature, and the other arts are natural companions to wine and food.

I know that some readers have taken our winery tour in Oakville. This one-hour learning experience, conducted by most knowledgeable hosts, shows how we grow grapes and produce wine in the Napa Valley and concludes with a tasting of representative wines, naturally accompanied by a sampling of food from the Vineyard Room.

When Rosa and my father, Cesare, immigrated to Virginia, Minnesota, shortly after the turn of the century, my father began working in the iron mines, but soon changed to running a boardinghouse for Italian immigrant workers. He and my mother also started a grocery store and a restaurant. The local Italian community, recognizing his ability in selecting fresh fruits and vegetables—and perhaps his business skills—sent him regularly to what was becoming regarded as the fruit basket of the nation, California. Grapes for winemaking were an integral part of those expeditions. He early recognized the superior vineyard areas of the Napa and San Joaquin valleys.

In Rosa's kitchen, especially after we moved to Lodi in 1923, I learned the difference that the freshest produce can make. This has been an enduring lesson, and it applies to winemaking as well. I express it at the winery with our motto, "Making good wine is a skill, fine wine an art."

On settling in the Napa Valley in 1943, my family began a campaign to create an appreciation for wine—our wine, Napa Valley wine, all California wine, truly all the world's wines. Education was and still is the key. Our progress has required enormous energy and deep commitment. In carrying out this mission, we have relied on the vision my parents instilled in all of us: to become the best in what we do; to live a quest for excellence.

So, my enduring memories of wine have been the tastes I learned at our family's table. My parents came to the United States from the town of Sassoferato in the Marches province on the eastern coast of Italy. Revisiting there a few years ago, I was reminded of the joy in tasting that I discovered as a boy in my mother's kitchen.

Those early pleasures of the table have been strengthened by the more sophisticated experiences of food and wine that I've enjoyed all over the world. Yet I hold a basic commitment to our local Napa Valley cuisine—as it was when I was a young man and as it is now—which I want to share through the pages of this book. My family and I encourage you to adopt some of this pleasurable lifestyle—what we call the good life—for yourselves. Please come with me to learn about the best we can offer.

ROBERT MONDAVI

THE HARVEST SHARED

TO GATHER AT TABLE WITH FAMILY AND FRIENDS

time-honored traditions that value family and community, with food and wine as partners that contribute to well-being and happiness. Just as they make every guest feel honored at their home, their winery, and the concerts and art exhibitions they sponsor, the Mondavis welcome readers and invite them to share an enthusiasm for food, wine, and a good life through this book.

To gather at table with family and friends, to enjoy food, wine, and life together is an act made up of many. In one sense, a community of people beyond those we know—farmers, vintners, warehouse workers, shippers, and others—makes it possible for all of us to find nourishment. The Mondavis, being both producers and consumers, have an intimate view of how important these connections are.

They understand how people—in the kinds of fruit and vegetables they plant, the cheese they make, the breads they bake—as well as the soil and sun create good food and wine. Their pleasure and mission has been to deepen their own understanding of the arts of the table and to share their insights with as many people as possible.

They have done this by including the communities of art and music, the community of fine local and international chefs, and their neighbors in the Napa Valley. Greeting 1,000-odd guests at the winery's twenty-fifth Fourth of July concert, they said simply, "We are so glad you could be here tonight. Enjoy the beautiful evening, the wonderful music of the Preservation Hall Jazz Band,

who have been with us twenty-four of the last twenty-five years, and celebrate being in this part of America." And so people did.

There are many ways to cultivate a good life of family, friends, food, and wine. The Mondavis believe the family is the most important element in fostering the sense of joy and pleasure that the table offers. Robert's and Margrit's early lives fostered an inclusive view of the relationships that make family. Robert says, "My family gave me the enduring values of moderation in eating and drinking, of balance rather than excess, and of comradeship."

As director of cultural affairs at the winery, Margrit lives the kind of busy schedule that many contemporary women follow. For her, it is all the more important to take time with the family at table—to exchange the little news of everyday life, to affirm the affections that keep us happy in life.

Robert and Margrit grew up in families that opened their doors to friends, acquaintances, and even strangers. Robert's mother, Rosa, was a legendary cook who delighted in having her home filled with people. Friends and family visited from around the United States and from Italy when Rosa and Robert's father, Cesare, settled in Minnesota. When they decided to move to California and try their hand at making wine, their circle of friends, acquaintances, and business associates widened. There was always something good to eat and drink—antipasto, a plate of cookies, or a bowl of homemade pasta, espresso, and wine. At the home of Margrit's mother and father, in the canton of Ticino, Switzerland, guests were always welcome. Depending on

"I find it takes as much time to order something to go, to pick it up, and to arrange it at home as it does to stop at the market and get a nice piece of fish or chicken I can poach, whatever produce is the best of the season, and a good loaf of bread. Somehow the food one prepares oneself, no matter how simple, is more nourishing to the spirit as well as the stomach. And cooking for the family is itself a relaxing activity."

—MARGRIT BIEVER MONDAVI

the hour, there would be pastries, a bowl of soup, which Margrit's mother made with seasonal vegetables from the garden, perhaps a blanquette de veau, and to drink, herb tea, coffee, and always wine.

Robert's children, Michael, Marcia, and Tim, have key responsibilities in the winery. Michael is chief executive officer, Marcia represents the winery in New York, and Tim is winemaker. One of Margrit's children, Annie Roberts, is chef at the

winery. They are naturally proud and happy that their children have chosen to work with them, and when they welcome guests to the many cultural events they sponsor, they always mention their "extended family," which includes the staff of the winery, most of whom have worked with them for years. And they count as extended family the many chefs who "have contributed so much to our understanding of food and wine." These are not only the stellar chefs who have participated in the winery's Great Chefs Program—Simone Beck, Georges Blanc, Julia Child, Marian Morash, Jacques Pépin, Wolfgang Puck, Jeremiah Tower, the Troisgros (Jean, Michel, and Pierre), Alice Waters, and Paula Wolfert, to mention just a few—but the many talented local chefs with whom they work.

Beyond the family, the Mondavis know that there are many avenues to increase our sense of connection to, and pleasure of, food and wine. Margrit and Robert keep a small kitchen garden, which provides the treats of

"It's good to rely on your memories, as long as you can be very open to surprises as well. There are great discoveries every time, especially when you guess wrong. For example, with some kinds of tropical spicy dishes that have fruit, herbs, and chilies, young red wines such as Merlot, Zinfandel, or Pinot Noir can be quite good, though we used to think white wines were the only ones possible. Food and wine pairing is actually quite versatile."

—MARGRIT BIEVER MONDAVI

the season: just-picked lettuces and herbs, tomatoes, beans, chili peppers. For those of us without that advantage, there are farmers' markets, which are making a comeback in many cities and towns. These markets offer not only a greater range of foodstuffs than most people can cultivate themselves, but also the opportunity to socialize with neighbors and friends.

To learn about wine—what you like with what food—the Mondavis recommend informal wine-tasting groups with friends. Hearing how others experience a wine's flavor can open your own perceptions. Over the years Robert has found that it's helpful to keep discovering the flavors that wine reveals, both with food and by itself. Friends and family can expand their knowledge and pleasure by listening to one another describe how each palate tastes wine. For Margrit our palates are not only quite individual, but change as well.

Eat what you like, and like what you eat; drink what you like, and like what you drink" are the Mondavi mottoes. Robert listens to what his body tells him about when, what, and how much to eat and drink. "Out of politeness I used to eat too much when I was invited out. At a certain point, I realized that I didn't do this at home; now, no matter what the occasion, I rely on my stomach to tell me when it is just satisfied. It's a good thing to trust your body and have confidence in it."

Most of us have had the experience of craving for a particular food. Paying attention to the reason for that hunger—were we stimulated by a commercial for Krispy Corn Chips or were we actually hungry?—can make a big dif-

"It is very interesting what you can learn, and humbling, because you come up against your preconceptions about what a wine should taste like, or what foods it goes with."

—ROBERT MONDAVI

ference in the way we eat. Margrit has found

that this kind of attention can be useful in

deciding what and how much to cook. "Our

bodies can tell us a lot; I cook less meat than I

used to because we are feeling well and healthy

without it."

Even more important than *what* we eat or

drink is an attitude of generosity toward the

people who share life with us, toward our-

selves, and toward food and wine, which nour-

ish and bring us pleasure. The Mondavis

believe that whatever you do, you can do with

a sense of sharing. In their lives, this impulse

has manifested itself in making the best wine

they can, and deepening their understanding of

how food and wine are civilizing aspects of life.

As Robert says, "One thing you'll notice about

giving is that it feels good."

A Note on the Recipes

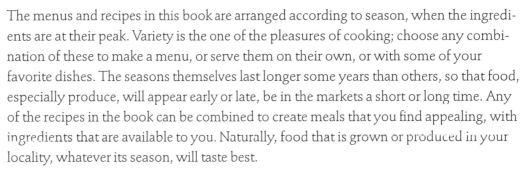

The menus and recipes in this book are arranged according to season, when the ingredients are at their peak. Variety is the one of the pleasures of cooking; choose any combination of these to make a menu, or serve them on their own, or with some of your favorite dishes. The seasons themselves last longer some years than others, so that food, especially produce, will appear early or late, be in the markets a short or long time. Any of the recipes in the book can be combined to create meals that you find appealing, with ingredients that are available to you. Naturally, food that is grown or produced in your locality, whatever its season, will taste best.

Recipes are, by their nature, interactive. It is part of the fun of cooking to make them your own, particularly by adjusting the seasonings—oils, vinegars, salt, herbs, and spices—so the dishes taste just as you like. Margrit looks to other cooks and their recipes for their insights into how ingredients can be combined and techniques refined. "I use recipes for ideas; tasting and tasting again is the most important thing to find the balance of flavors."

In these recipes, all eggs are large. Flour is all-purpose unbleached, unless otherwise specified. Vegetables are medium-size, unless otherwise called for. Medium-size onions, bell peppers, and tomatoes weigh about 6 ounces each, carrots about 4 ounces.

IN THE NAPA VALLEY AUTUMN IS

AUTUMN

THE SEASON OF GREAT ANTICIPATION

but in the Napa Valley autumn is the season of great anticipation. Vineyard owners, grape pickers, and all those who work to make wine from grapes are watching the sky and waiting for the grapes to reach their full potential. For winemakers this is the time of crucial decision: when to pick each variety of grape. It is a decision that has to be made anew every autumn, as it has been from ancient times, and most winemakers agree that it is as much art as experience. As the grapes ripen, they are tested for sugars, yeasts, and pH. They are tasted and tasted again, daily, and sometimes even hourly.

For even if winemakers study winemaking in the world's finest wine-growing regions, and use the best scientific analytic tests as the Mondavis do, the vintners' primary job is to know the character of their grapes well. As Tim Mondavi says, "We have worked on evolving methods and techniques to let the grapes express themselves as wine, to do as little as possible with the wines and let them make themselves."

While the drama of the harvest is unfolding and the roads are full of gondolas loaded with grapes, the tomatoes are reaching their most flavorful state. Gardens and farmers' markets are full of sweet and hot peppers, eggplants, squash, melons, basil, marjoram, oregano,

marigolds, zinnias, and sunflowers. Pumpkins and winter squash are swelling for later harvest. Meals tend to be simple, centered around fresh produce and often the grill. As long as the weather is warm, refreshing wines such as Fumé Blanc, Johannisberg Riesling, and light styles of Chardonnay, Pinot Noir, and Zinfandel are served.

From mid-October to early November the nights begin to chill, and sometimes the days as well. Local apples, pears, and table grapes

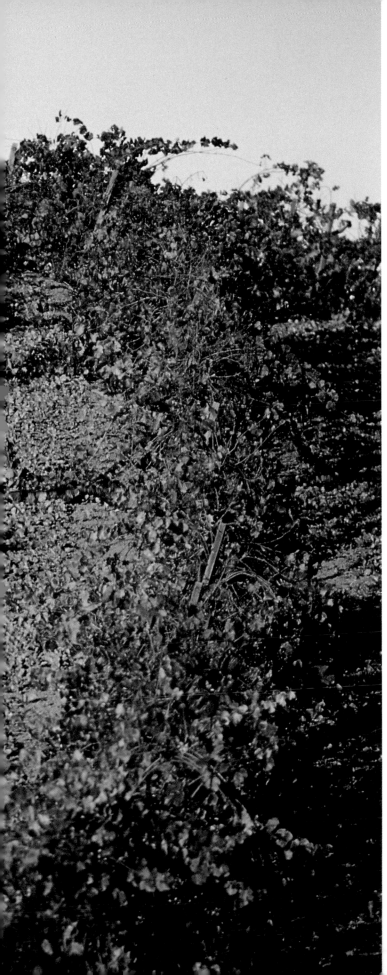

appear on tables and in dishes, taking the place of summer's berries. Farmers bring spinach, chard, and radicchio from the cool coast a few miles away. People turn to heartier foods, and use the oven more than the grill. More robust wines, such as Reserve Chardonnay, Pinot Noir, and Cabernet Sauvignon, are served. Winemakers have largely finished with harvest decisions and concentrate on tasting the juice from tanks and fermenters to decide when to press. The pace slows with the shortening days, as it has done for thousands of years wherever grapes have been cultivated and turned into wine.

Blessing of the Grapes Lunch at the Vineyard Room

Sangria

Guacamole

Shrimp and Jicama Salad

WHITE ZINFANDEL

Grilled Chicken with Mexican Spices

Black Beans with Jalapeños

Rice with Tomatoes

CHARDONNAY AND PINOT NOIR

Cinnamon Ice Cream
with Fresh Tropical Fruit

MOSCATO D'ORO

The tradition of blessing each year's harvest has been honored since the winery opened; no other ceremony so exemplifies the Mondavis' philosophy of the particular blend of agriculture and art that is winemaking. Tim Mondavi says, "Someone above watches and allows us to do our best with these fruits of the earth."

The Carmelite Monastery is a neighbor of the winery's, situated on the hill behind the vineyards. Father Edward and Brother Charles of the monastery say the simple and heartfelt words of the blessing: "The earth has yielded its fruit. Our Lord God has blessed us. Bless the fruits of our labor. May our hands work holy works in our lives." In his brief ecumenical remarks, Father Edward notes that some form of grape blessing has existed for thousands of years,

and cites the Jewish tradition of blessing grapes and wine. He repeats the truth that all those who grow plants know: Mother Earth supports and sustains all life; humans are stewards of the bounty that comes from water and soil.

The ceremonies include the family's thanks to the women and men who harvest the grapes, those who work at the winery, and the other vineyard owners who provide a part of the winery's grapes. At the conclusion, Father Edwards blesses the gondolas of grapes, and everyone present. Tim signals the excitement about the harvest's possibilities by saying, "I believe this is going to be a great vintage," and tosses bunches of sun-warmed, sweet-tart Chardonnay grapes to the guests.

The Annie Roberts menu for the lunch following the blessing pays tribute to the Mexican heritage of many who work to bring in and process the harvest. It also shows that spicy food and wine can be good partners. To accompany the guacamole and chips, Annie made a sangria with Zinfandel and citrus fruit, showing how complementary grapes and citrus can be. With the refreshing, mildly spicy shrimp and jicama salad, a White Zinfandel brings out the slight sweetness and crispness of the jicama. Many people who like both wine and chilies find Chardonnay is the best match for the fire in the chilies. Pinot Noir fans are not neglected, with a glass of their favorite wine to enjoy with the mesquite-grilled chicken, beans, and rice with chilies and spices. The cinnamon ice cream and fruit, served with Moscato d'Oro, ends the warm autumn day's lunch with a light, silky treat for the palate.

SANGRIA

When you're serving a large party, you can easily double or triple the recipe. This sangria relies on the natural sugars in the wine and fruit for its sweetness; some palates may prefer to add a little sugar.

1   BOTTLE (750 ML) ZINFANDEL OR OTHER FULL-BODIED RED WINE
1   CUP FRESHLY SQUEEZED ORANGE JUICE
JUICE OF 1 LEMON, OR TO TASTE
½   ORANGE, SLICED VERY THIN
½   LIME, SLICED VERY THIN
½   LEMON, SLICED VERY THIN

Pour the wine into a pitcher or serving bowl. Stir in the orange and lemon juice. Chill the sangria for at least an hour before serving. When ready to serve, float the orange, lime, and lemon slices on top.

ANNIE'S GUACAMOLE

This pure and simple, rather mild guacamole is one Annie makes every year because everyone who has tasted it clamors for it again. The flavor is well balanced and goes well with sangria (preceding recipe) and simple warm-weather wines such as White Zinfandel.

6   GREEN ONIONS, WITH 3 OR 4 INCHES OF GREEN, SLICED THIN
2   JALAPEÑO PEPPERS, SEEDED AND DICED FINE
ABOUT 8 OUNCES RIPE TOMATOES, CORED AND DICED FINE
2   GARLIC CLOVES, MINCED
ABOUT ⅓ CUP CHOPPED FRESH CILANTRO LEAVES
4   OR 5 HASS AVOCADOS, ABOUT 2½ POUNDS
ABOUT ¼ CUP LIME JUICE
1   TEASPOON SALT, OR TO TASTE

Combine the green onions, jalapeños, tomatoes, garlic, and cilantro in a bowl. Peel, seed, and dice the avocados and add to the bowl. Mash the avocados slightly and mix well with the other ingredients. Stir in the lime juice and salt. Cover the guacamole and let it stand for 10 or 15 minutes. Adjust the seasoning with lime juice and/or salt and serve.

SHRIMP AND JICAMA SALAD

To make a casual summer dinner, serve the salad as an accompaniment to Grilled Chicken with Mexican Spices (recipe follows), along with some warm tortillas, guacamole, and corn chips. The vinaigrette and salad may be prepared ahead before grilling the shrimp. It takes about 5 minutes to grill the shrimp and dress the salad.

MARINADE AND SHRIMP

- 2 TEASPOONS MINCED LEMON ZEST
- 1 LARGE GARLIC CLOVE, MINCED
- 1 TO 2 JALAPEÑO PEPPERS, SEEDED AND DICED FINE
- 1 TABLESPOON MINCED FRESH CILANTRO LEAVES
- ¼ CUP OLIVE OIL
- 1½ POUNDS MEDIUM SHRIMP, SHELLED AND DEVEINED

Mix the lemon zest, garlic, jalapeños, cilantro, and olive oil together in a bowl. Add the shrimp and marinate in the refrigerator for 2 to 8 hours, stirring occasionally.

VINAIGRETTE AND SALAD

- ½ RED ONION, ABOUT 4 OUNCES, CUT IN SMALL DICE
- 1 TABLESPOON CHOPPED FRESH CILANTRO LEAVES
- 2 TABLESPOONS CHAMPAGNE VINEGAR OR WHITE WINE VINEGAR
- 1 TABLESPOON LIME JUICE
- ½ CUP OLIVE OIL
- ½ TEASPOON SALT
- 1 HEAD ROMAINE LETTUCE, ABOUT 12 OUNCES
- ABOUT 6 OUNCES RIPE TOMATOES, PREFERABLY PLUM, DICED SMALL
- ABOUT 8 OUNCES JICAMA, PEELED AND JULIENNED

Combine the onion, cilantro, vinegar, and lime juice in a bowl. Whisk in the olive oil to make an emulsion. Add the salt.

Trim and clean the lettuce, reserving the large outer leaves for another use. Dry the lettuce and arrange it on a serving platter.

TO FINISH THE SALAD

Remove the shrimp from the refrigerator about 30 minutes before you're ready to cook it. Let stand while you prepare a medium-hot grill.

Thread the shrimp loosely on skewers and grill until they are just done, about 1½ minutes on each side. Remove the shrimp from the skewers to a dish and drizzle them with about 2 tablespoons of the vinaigrette.

(continued)

Drizzle about 2 tablespoons of the vinaigrette over the lettuce. Toss the remaining vinaigrette with the tomatoes and jicama. Mound the tomatoes and jícama on the lettuce and arrange the shrimp on the salad. Serve immediately.

GRILLED CHICKEN WITH MEXICAN SPICES   SERVES 8

Whether Annie Roberts is preparing grilled chicken for entertaining at home, or for many people in the Vineyard Room, she usually grills the chicken about 10 minutes to give it flavor and color, then finishes the cooking in the oven. The chicken will have especially fine flavor if you grill it over mesquite or another hardwood charcoal.

2 BROILER CHICKENS, 2½ TO 2¾ POUNDS EACH

1 TABLESPOON CUMIN SEEDS, LIGHTLY TOASTED IN A SMALL SKILLET AND GROUND

2 TEASPOONS DRIED OREGANO, PREFERABLY MEXICAN, LIGHTLY TOASTED IN A SMALL SKILLET AND CRUMBLED

1 TABLESPOON CORIANDER SEED, LIGHTLY TOASTED IN A SMALL SKILLET AND GROUND

3 GARLIC CLOVES

1 TO 2 TABLESPOONS LIME JUICE

1 TEASPOON SALT

Split the chickens in half along the breast and backbone, or have the butcher do this. Rinse the chickens well, and pat dry.

Combine the cumin, oregano, and coriander in a small bowl. Press the garlic into the bowl, or mince it fine and add it to the bowl. Add enough lime juice to make a medium-dense paste. Stir in the salt.

Loosen the skin of the chicken and rub the marinade between the skin and the flesh. Let the chicken marinate for an hour at cool room temperature, or up to 4 hours in the refrigerator.

Remove the chicken from the refrigerator 30 minutes before grilling. Let stand while you prepare a medium-hot grill.

Grill the chicken, bone side down, for 5 minutes. Turn and grill skin side down for 5 minutes. When the chicken has a nice golden brown color and grill marks, you may finish cooking it in a preheated 400° F oven for 15 to 20 minutes, or until the juices run clear. Or finish the chicken on the grill, turning frequently, until the juices run clear. Let the chicken stand for 10 or 15 minutes before cutting the pieces in half and serving.

Black Beans with Jalapeños

These black beans are meant to be mildly spicy; taste your jalapeños and decrease the amount if they are very hot. The amount of vegetables in the recipe makes the beans rather fresh and light tasting. They are good as an accompaniment to grilled meats, and as a base for burritos, tostadas, and enchiladas. They are complemented by several wines: Pinot Noir, Zinfandel, Merlot, even a full-bodied Chardonnay, if that is your preference.

1   POUND DRIED BLACK BEANS, RINSED AND SORTED

1   LARGE ONION, DICED

1   SMALL GREEN BELL PEPPER, DICED

1   GARLIC CLOVE, MINCED

¼   CUP OLIVE OIL

1½ TABLESPOONS CUMIN SEEDS, LIGHTLY TOASTED IN A SMALL SKILLET AND GROUND

1   TABLESPOON DRIED OREGANO, PREFERABLY MEXICAN

1   TEASPOON TABASCO

¼   CUP FINE-DICED JALAPEÑO PEPPERS

1   TEASPOON SALT

ABOUT 10 OUNCES RIPE PLUM TOMATOES, DICED

1   CUP CHICKEN BROTH

1   CUP GRATED QUESO FRESCO OR MONTEREY JACK CHEESE

Soak the beans overnight in water to cover. Drain, rinse, and place in a 6- to 8-quart pot. Cover with about 2 inches of water. Cover the pot, bring the beans to a boil, reduce the heat to a simmer, and cook until just tender, 45 to 60 minutes. Drain the beans, reserving the cooking liquid, and return them to the pot.

Sauté the onion, green pepper, and garlic in the olive oil for about 5 minutes. Stir in the cumin, oregano, Tabasco, jalapeños, and salt and cook for a minute or two. Stir in the tomatoes.

Add the mixture to the beans, along with the chicken broth and 1 cup of the reserved bean cooking liquid. Cook the beans 15 minutes or so, until they are tender but still hold their shape. Add more bean liquid if necessary, and adjust the seasoning.

Serve hot, garnished with the grated cheese, or pass the cheese in a separate dish.

RICE WITH TOMATOES

If ripe, fresh tomatoes aren't available, use a 14-ounce can of plum tomatoes; you will not need all the juice from the can. Long-grain rice may be used in place of medium-grain; it will take a little less time to cook after the broth is added. If the broth you use is already salted, you will probably need to decrease the amount of salt. The rice has a bit of southwestern/Mexican flavor because of the coriander, cumin, and cilantro, but it can accompany many simple grilled main courses of fish, chicken, or pork.

5 TABLESPOONS UNSALTED BUTTER

1 ONION, DICED

1 TEASPOON CORIANDER SEEDS, LIGHTLY TOASTED IN A SMALL SKILLET AND GROUND

1 TEASPOON CUMIN SEEDS, LIGHTLY TOASTED IN A SMALL SKILLET AND GROUND

2 CUPS MEDIUM-GRAIN RICE, SUCH AS ARBORIO

3 CUPS CHICKEN BROTH

½ CUP DRY WHITE WINE

2 GARLIC CLOVES, CHOPPED FINE

12 OUNCES RIPE TOMATOES, PEELED, SEEDED, AND DICED

About 2 TEASPOONS SALT

3 TABLESPOONS CHOPPED FRESH CILANTRO LEAVES

Place a saucepan over medium heat and melt the butter. Add the onion, coriander, and cumin, and soften. When the onion has a nice golden brown color, add the rice, mix well, and cook for about 7 minutes, stirring occasionally.

While the rice is cooking, bring the broth and wine to a simmer in a small saucepan. Add the garlic and tomatoes to the rice and cook for 1 minute. Add the hot broth and salt and stir well. Reduce the heat to low, cover, and cook for 15 minutes. Turn the heat off and let the rice stand, covered, for 10 minutes before serving. Stir in the cilantro just before serving.

CINNAMON ICE CREAM
WITH FRESH TROPICAL FRUIT

For a more pronounced cinnamon flavor, which is good if you'd like to serve the ice cream with chocolate cake, add an extra cinnamon stick.

ICE CREAM

- **2 CUPS WHIPPING CREAM**
- **2 CUPS MILK**
- **1 CUP SUGAR**
- **3-INCH PIECE CINNAMON STICK**
- **2 LARGE EGG YOLKS**
- **1 TEASPOON PURE VANILLA EXTRACT**

Combine the cream, milk, sugar, and cinnamon stick in a saucepan. Bring to a boil, stirring frequently. Reduce the heat to a simmer and cook for 5 minutes. Remove from the heat and let steep 15 to 20 minutes. Remove the cinnamon stick.

Beat the egg yolks lightly in a bowl. Slowly stir in about ½ cup of the hot cream mixture, then slowly whisk the egg mixture into the saucepan. Cook the mixture, stirring frequently, until the custard just coats the back of a metal spoon, about 3 minutes. Do not allow the mixture to boil.

Strain the custard into a metal bowl and stir in the vanilla. Set the bowl in a larger bowl half filled with ice water and chill the mixture thoroughly, stirring occasionally, then place in the freezer or refrigerator. When the mixture is very cold, pour it into an ice cream maker and freeze according to manufacturer's instructions.

FRUIT

2 OR 3 KINDS OF ASSORTED SEASONAL TROPICAL AND LOCAL FRUIT,
   SUCH AS SMALL BANANAS, FRESH MANGOES, PAPAYAS, AND BERRIES

Just before serving the ice cream, slice and/or wash enough fruit so that each dish of ice cream has 2 or 3 pieces of each kind. Serve the ice cream slightly soft, surrounded by the fruit.

Fireside Dinner

Fresh Avocado Soup

FUMÉ BLANC

Roast Chicken Stuffed with Swiss Chard

CHARDONNAY AND PINOT NOIR

Swiss Chard with Swiss Cheese

Chestnut Vacherin

Taleggio, Sonoma Lamb, and Cantal Cheeses

CABERNET SAUVIGNON

For Margrit and Robert, having friends or family to share a meal with them is always a chance to make people happy. Margrit says, "We enjoy casual entertaining that gives us time with our guests. I like to make everything special beforehand, so that our guests feel just a bit spoiled, and so I can be with them. In autumn, I'll find the nicest gourds at the farmers' market, or branches of fall-colored leaves from our garden or friends', or chestnut prunings with the nuts still in their prickly cases. I've collected hand-crafted chickens, ducks, frogs, and rabbits of wood, ceramic, reeds, and metal during our travels and from local artisans to set the table in a way that brings people pleasure. It's nicest when the table, as well as the menu, is in keeping with the season. Whatever the occasion or time of year, I so enjoy drawing the menus at the last minute, when all the elements of people, food, and wine come together to inspire me.

One of our favorite customs during autumn and winter is to serve a light first course of soup in front of the fireplace. If we have a glass of our Sparkling Brut Reserve with a bit of toast, salmon, and capers, we often don't serve wine with the soup. Sometimes, though, we'll begin with soup and serve Fumé Blanc. I'm very fond of Swiss chard in this season, and like the way it tastes with the chicken. The

chicken and vegetable course take care of themselves in the oven while we are talking by the fire. I usually finish assembling the vacherin before the guests arrive. In this menu, it's interesting to serve a taste of Chardonnay and Pinot Noir with the chicken, so people can decide which they like best with it. We are fortunate to have some excellent cheese purveyors here in the valley. On a cold autumn night, nothing is as good as a little plate of fine cheese and a glass of lovely Reserve Cabernet Sauvignon."

Robert says, "Living well, by which I mean being with others as much as with yourself, is about finding the harmony that exists, taking the time to make good food and wine, and to enjoy them." They choose the food and wine to make everyone at ease, like this dinner for food and wine friends—simple, yet complex enough to offer the opportunity for observations. But when the grandchildren come over, homemade french fries, a fresh fish dish, and salad are on the menu, with easy wines for the adults. As Margrit puts it, "For me, it is so important for the family to be relaxed over simple home-cooked food, so they can exchange tidbits of what they did during the day."

FRESH AVOCADO SOUP

In mid- to late autumn, the California avocado harvest is at its peak. Most avocados are grown in southern California, but some enterprising ranchers grow them in Watsonville, just north of Monterey on the coast. Because of the colder climate, the avocados must stay on the trees for eighteen months before harvest, rather than the twelve months typical of southern California. This extra maturing time gives them a full, rich flavor.

The vegetable and light herb flavors in this soup make a good match with a Fumé Blanc. The base broth with vegetables can be prepared a day ahead and reheated. Just before serving, add the avocados.

2 MEDIUM-SIZE CARROTS, PEELED

1 MEDIUM-SIZE ONION

2 MEDIUM-SIZE CELERY STALKS

2 TABLESPOONS UNSALTED BUTTER

6 CUPS CHICKEN BROTH

3 GARLIC CLOVES, PEELED

3 FRESH ITALIAN PARSLEY SPRIGS

2 LARGE FIRM-RIPE HASS AVOCADOS, ABOUT 8 OUNCES EACH

2 TO 3 TABLESPOONS SHERRY

SALT

Dice the carrots, onion, and celery fine. Soften the vegetables in the butter over medium heat in a soup pot. Add the chicken broth, garlic, and parsley. Bring to a boil and reduce the heat to a simmer. Cook for about 30 minutes; remove the garlic and parsley.

When ready to serve, peel and seed the avocados and cut them in about ½-inch dice. Add the avocados and sherry to the soup and just heat through. Adjust the seasoning and serve hot, in mugs.

ROAST CHICKEN STUFFED WITH SWISS CHARD

The chicken and stuffing may be prepared early in the day and refrigerated until an hour and a half before cooking. Stuff the chickens when you are ready to roast them. Reserve the chard leaves to make Swiss Chard with Swiss Cheese (recipe follows), a natural partner to this dish.

Margrit's tip: To flatten the chickens, which allows them to cook more quickly, just give a quick, solid whack with the flat of a cleaver so you don't break the skin. The breast bones of these small chickens are quite soft.

- 2 CHICKENS, 2½ TO 2¾ POUNDS EACH
- SALT AND FRESH GROUND PEPPER
- 1 BUNCH SWISS CHARD, ABOUT 12 OUNCES, STEMS ONLY, WASHED AND CUT IN ¼-INCH DICE
- 1 MEDIUM-SIZE ONION, DICED FINE
- 4 OUNCES MUSHROOMS, CLEANED, TRIMMED, AND CHOPPED
- 2 GARLIC CLOVES, MINCED
- 3 OR 4 FRESH BASIL LEAVES, CHOPPED FINE
- 1 FRESH ITALIAN PARSLEY SPRIG, LEAVES CHOPPED FINE
- 2 TABLESPOONS OLIVE OIL
- ½ CUP FRESH BREAD CRUMBS
- 2 LARGE EGGS, LIGHTLY BEATEN
- ½ CUP DRY RICOTTA CHEESE, GRATED

Rinse the chickens and pat dry. Place the chickens, breast up, on a cutting board. With the flat of a meat cleaver, break the breastbones and ribs. Season the chickens inside and out with salt and pepper. Preheat the oven to 375° F.

Sauté the chard stems, onion, mushrooms, garlic, basil, and parsley in the olive oil in a sauté pan until the vegetables are slightly softened, about 5 minutes.

Remove from the heat and stir in the bread crumbs, eggs, and ricotta cheese. Season lightly with salt and pepper. Divide the mixture in half.

Gently loosen the skin over the chicken breast, beginning at the neck. Gently work the stuffing under the skin. Repeat the procedure with the second chicken and batch of stuffing.

Place each chicken in a baking dish or roasting pan and roast for 50 minutes to an hour, until the juices run clear when the thigh joint is pierced. If the chicken becomes too brown near the end of roasting, cover lightly with aluminum foil.

Remove the chickens from the oven and let stand for 5 to 10 minutes. Cut the chicken in quarters and serve some of the stuffing with each portion.

SWISS CHARD WITH SWISS CHEESE

Swiss chard has a slightly nutty flavor that goes well with many vegetables and legumes, and most fish, meat, and poultry. It will harmonize with any wine you are serving.

2   BUNCHES SWISS CHARD, ABOUT 1 ½ POUNDS, WASHED

4   TABLESPOONS UNSALTED BUTTER

½   CUP SHREDDED GRUYÈRE CHEESE

FRESH-GROUND PEPPER

OPTIONAL GARNISH: CHERRY TOMATOES, HALVED

Remove the stems from the chard and reserve them for another use. Select 8 of the best-looking leaves and set aside. Cut the remaining chard into about 1-inch shreds.

Preheat the oven to 375° F. Lightly butter eight 5- to 6-ounce custard cups or small baking dishes.

Blanch the chard leaves for about 1½ minutes. Drain, refresh with cold water, drain again, and layer one each in the prepared custard cups. Blanch the shredded chard about 1½ minutes, and drain.

Melt the butter in a small saucepan over medium-low heat and bring it to a hazelnut color. Toss the butter with the shredded chard in a bowl, then divide the mixture among the lined custard cups.

Sprinkle the cheese over the chard and season lightly with pepper. Place the chard dishes on a baking sheet and bake for about 20 minutes, until the cheese is just melted and bubbling. Unmold the chard onto serving plates or a platter. Garnish with several halved cherry tomatoes, if desired. Serve immediately.

Chestnut Vacherin

Margrit's tip: The vacherin is crispest when it is served about 30 minutes after assembling, though it will hold for a couple of hours. The meringues will store a day or two packed between brown or wax paper in airtight containers. To make the circles, use a plate, pan, or lid for the outline.

MERINGUE

PARCHMENT PAPER

6 LARGE EGG WHITES, AT ROOM TEMPERATURE

PINCH OF SALT

⅛ TEASPOON CREAM OF TARTAR

1½ CUPS MINUS 1 TABLESPOON SUGAR

Preheat the oven to 225° F. Cut two sheets of parchment paper at least 18 inches long and 13 inches wide. Outline 8-inch circles on the parchment with a pencil, then lightly butter the parchment. Line two baking sheets, at least 17 inches long and 12 inches, wide with the parchment, buttered side down.

In a bowl and using an electric mixer, beat the egg whites until foamy. Add the salt and cream of tartar and beat to soft peaks. Add the sugar, about ⅓ cup at time, until the meringue has formed stiff peaks.

Divide the meringue into four portions. Using a cake spatula, spread each parchment circle with one portion of the meringue. Or, pipe the meringue through a pastry bag fitted with a large plain tip.

Bake the meringues 1 hour and 20 minutes, changing shelves halfway through the baking. The meringues should be firm to a light touch with your finger, and very lightly colored. Turn the oven off and let the meringues stand for 5 minutes with the oven door ajar.

Remove the parchment sheets to racks and cool the meringues to room temperature.

FILLING

1 JAR (16 OUNCES) PEELED CHESTNUTS

ABOUT 1 CUP MILK

⅓ CUP LIGHT KARO SYRUP

2 TABLESPOONS KIRSCH

1½ OUNCES BEST-QUALITY MILK CHOCOLATE

2 CUPS WHIPPING CREAM

Put the chestnuts in a saucepan and barely cover with milk. Bring to a simmer and cook about 10 minutes, until the chestnuts are very tender.

Drain the chestnuts, reserving the milk, and put them in a food processor. Add the syrup and Kirsch and process the chestnuts to a puree. If the puree is very dense, add a little milk.

Shave the milk chocolate with a vegetable peeler. Whip the cream to firm peaks.

To Finish the Vacherin

Peel the parchment from the meringues and place one meringue on a serving dish. Lightly spread one quarter of the chestnut puree over the meringue. Spread one quarter of the whipped cream over the puree. Finish layering the vacherin, ending with whipped cream. Sprinkle the chocolate shavings over the top.

To serve, cut the vacherin with a serrated knife.

A Julia Child Lunch for the Great Chefs

at the Robert Mondavi Winery

Spinach Quiche

FUMÉ BLANC

Mediterranean Fish Stew with Rouille

PINOT NOIR

Le Brantôme (French Walnut Layer Cake)

SAUVIGNON BLANC BOTRYTIS

Those who participate in the Great Chefs program at the Robert Mondavi Winery agree that the whole is greater than the parts. And when the parts include the finest chefs in the world—acknowledged masters of the art and craft of cooking as well as the rising stars—fine wines chosen by the chefs to complement the dishes they demonstrate and serve, in a setting of natural and human-created beauty, the whole is great indeed.

Axel Fabré, director of the program, works every year to bring these key elements together, and to enhance them with thematic seasonal motifs, music and art, special table service, seminars relating to the dining arts, and educational wine tastings. Axel, with her fine sense of style and inimitable French accent, brings a real feeling of festivity to the program, which she describes as a "feast for all the senses."

Gary Jenanyan, executive chef of the program, oversees the many details of kitchen operation. His work of finding the freshest seasonal ingredients and creating a team of guest chefs and staff is the essence of every true chef's vocation, the desire to make people happy by feeding them harmoniously. Gary's relaxed manner and sense of humor contribute to the convivial atmosphere of the program.

obert and Margrit greet the guests at every program, as they have since 1976, when the program began. It is personally important for them to share their belief that great food and fine wine are best enjoyed and appreciated together. Robert says, "The table provides one of life's great pleasures. Dining allows people the opportunity to savor each other's company, to develop and refine the art of conversation, to slow down and get in touch with the sensory aspects of life."

ulia Child has known and worked with Robert and Margrit for many years, in, as she says ". . . a pleasant and wonderful relationship. Bob and I share an interest in the professional aspects of food and wine, and to further these professions in our country, we cofounded the American Institute of Wine and Food. Margrit and I first met through my colleague Simone Beck, in southern France in the early 1960s. I've been participating in the Great Chefs program for some fifteen years, and I'm always glad to be here for that very special Mondavi combination of love and enthusiasm for food and wine, as well as for their genuine hospitality that extends to all the chefs and guests."

s part of her demonstration, Julia presented the following lunch menu, which illustrates her philosophy that moderation is the key to eating and living well. About her first course Julia said, "Most people do not have medical reasons for never eating eggs or butter. If they would eat a sensible portion of a well-made dish with good eggs and butter, they would be satisfied, and possibly happy. The quiche was in vogue for a while, then so badly made, with inferior crusts and too much cheese and filling, that it fell from favor."

Everyone who tasted Julia's quiche can understand why she is an acknowledged master chef. The crust is sublimely flaky, and the filling light, balanced, and flavorful. Not only because of her deep understanding of how ingredients relate to each other, and how people and food relate, but in her unaffected ease, her unmistakable high-pitched voice, her unflagging energy, and her wit is Julia our best-known and -loved chef.

SPINACH QUICHE

Julia has an easy-to-remember formula for making quiche custard. "You can't be exact about total amounts, since pie shells vary in depth, but you can always calculate the custard by egg, using this formula: Whisk 1 egg in a measuring cup, and blend milk or other liquid to reach the ½ cup mark." As for the quiche shell, bake it in a 8- or 8½-inch tart shell with removable bottom at least ½ inch deep, or in a 9-inch pie plate. You will need more dough and custard if you use a pie plate. Since the crust is very buttery, use a baking sheet under a tart shell with removable bottom. Bake the shell so that it has time to cool to room temperature before filling with the custard.

3 LARGE EGGS

ABOUT 1 CUP MILK

1 PACKAGE (10 OUNCES) FRESH SPINACH

2 TABLESPOONS CHOPPED SHALLOTS OR SCALLIONS

2 TABLESPOONS UNSALTED BUTTER

¼ CUP GRATED SWISS CHEESE

1 PREBAKED QUICHE SHELL FROM JULIA'S PROCESSOR PIE DOUGH (RECIPE FOLLOWS)

SALT AND FRESH-GROUND PEPPER AND -GRATED NUTMEG

Beat the eggs lightly in a 2-cup measuring cup. Add enough milk to reach the 1½-cup mark. Set the custard aside.

Stem, wash, blanch, squeeze dry, then chop the spinach. Sauté the shallots or scallions briefly in the butter in a medium-size sauté pan. Add the spinach and stir over medium heat for several minutes until very tender. Remove from the heat and season carefully with salt, pepper, and a speck of nutmeg.

Preheat the oven to 375° F and place the rack in the upper-third level.

Spread half of the cheese in the prebaked quiche shell. Spread the spinach mixture over the cheese. Top with the remaining cheese. Beat the reserved custard briefly and pour it over the spinach, filling the shell to within ⅛ inch of its rim, if it is straight sided, and not much more than halfway if the shell is slant sided or the sides seem at all fragile.

Bake the quiche for 25 to 30 minutes, until the filling is lightly puffed and nicely browned. Cool the quiche for at least 10 minutes on a rack at room temperature before cutting and serving.

Julia's Processor Pie Dough
MAKES TWO 8- TO 8½-INCH TART SHELLS, OR ONE 9-INCH COVERED PIE

"Before the invention of the electric food processor," says Julia, "pie dough was certainly the nemesis and utter terror of many a cook, and the country abounded in tough crusts of every description. Now, with the food processor, dough making is as easy as pie, and this is top-quality dough at its buttery best." She adds this ahead-of-time note: "The pastry will keep under refrigeration for a day or two, but if you have used unbleached flour, which is preferred, it will gradually turn gray. For longer storage use the freezer, where it will keep perfectly for months, waiting to serve you."

3½ CUPS (1 POUND) UNBLEACHED ALL-PURPOSE FLOUR

2 TEASPOONS SALT

1¼ CUPS (10 OUNCES) CHILLED UNSALTED BUTTER, QUARTERED LENGTHWISE AND DICED

4 TABLESPOONS CHILLED VEGETABLE SHORTENING

⅔ TO 1 CUP ICE WATER

Have all ingredients measured out and ready to use. Place the flour, salt, and diced butter in the container of the processor and pulse five to six times in 1-second bursts to break up the butter. Add the shortening, turn on the machine, and immediately pour in ½ cup of ice water, pulsing two or three times. Remove the cover and feel the dough: it should look like a bunch of small lumps, and when you press a handful together the lumps should mass; if too dry, pulse more water in, in droplets. Do not overmix; the dough should not mass on the blade, but should hold together when pressed.

Turn the dough out onto your work surface, and with the heel, not the warm palm, of your hand, rapidly and roughly smear the dough by 3-spoonful bits 6 to 8 inches out on your work surface. This accomplishes the final blending of fat and flour. If the pastry seems stiff, sprinkle on more droplets of ice water as you smear, but do not overdo! Press the dough rapidly into a rough cake, wrap in a sheet of plastic, place in a plastic bag, and chill.

The dough should be chilled for at least an hour, preferably 2 hours or up to overnight, before using. This allows the flour particles to absorb the liquid and will make for a more tender dough; it also allow the butter to congeal for easy rolling.

To Form and Prebake a Quiche or Pie Shell

Divide the dough in half and roll out one portion about ⅛ inch thick. Place the dough in a tart shell or pie plate, trim or flute the edges, and prick the bottom at ¼-inch intervals with a table fork. Line the dough with aluminum foil and weight down with dried beans. Bake in a preheated 450° F oven for about 10 minutes, until the dough has set; remove the foil and beans and bake another 7 or 8 minutes to brown lightly.

MEDITERRANEAN FISH STEW WITH ROUILLE

Julia describes this delicious soup/stew as "an informal bouillabaisse you can make any-where that you can buy lean chowder-type fish. It's really the colorful and hearty soup base that counts here, so full of flavor you can even serve it as is, or substitute pasta, potatoes, beans, or chicken for fish."

The soup base can be made several days ahead and kept in the refrigerator. The rouille can be made a day or so ahead. Julia's directions for dry-toasted croutons stress choosing a country-style French or Italian bread with good body. Slice the bread about ¾ inch thick and place on a baking sheet. Dry the bread in a 325° F oven for 25 to 30 minutes, or until golden brown and crisp throughout.

ALL-PURPOSE MEDITERRANEAN SOUP BASE (RECIPE FOLLOWS)

2 TO 2½ POUNDS LEAN FISH, SKINLESS AND BONELESS, CUT INTO 2-INCH CHUNKS
 (COD, HAKE, HALIBUT, SEA BASS, MONKFISH, CATFISH, SNAPPER—A VARIETY IS PREFERABLE)

2 TO 3 DRY-TOASTED CROUTONS PER SERVING (SEE ABOVE)

ROUILLE (RECIPE FOLLOWS)

1 CUP CHOPPED FRESH PARSLEY

SALT AND FRESH-GROUND PEPPER

OPTIONAL GARNISH: GRATED PARMESAN OR HARD JACK CHEESE

When ready to prepare the soup, complete the soup base or take it from the refrigerator and bring it to a gentle boil over medium heat.

Add the fish and cook for 2 or 3 minutes, just until the fish is opaque rather than translucent and lightly springy to the touch. Correct the seasoning.

Place the dry-toasted croutons in warmed wide soup plates, top them with a spoonful of the rouille, ladle on the fish, then the soup. Finish with a generous sprinkling of parsley, and grated cheese, if desired. Pass the additional rouille separately.

All-Purpose Mediterranean Soup Base

½ CUP EXTRA-VIRGIN OLIVE OIL

2 CUPS SLICED ONIONS

8 LARGE GARLIC CLOVES, UNPEELED AND CHOPPED

3 CUPS CHOPPED FRESH TOMATOES, CORED BUT UNPEELED

2 CUPS CANNED ITALIAN PLUM TOMATOES

½ TEASPOON DRIED THYME

¼ TEASPOON FENNEL SEEDS

3 PINCHES SAFFRON THREADS, OR ¼ TEASPOON TURMERIC

1 3 x 1-INCH PIECE DRIED FRESH ORANGE PEEL, OR ½ TEASPOON BOTTLED DRIED PEEL

2 QUARTS LIQUID (FISH STOCK, WATER PLUS BOTTLED CLAM JUICE, OR A LIGHT CHICKEN BROTH)

SALT AND FRESH-GROUND PEPPER

Pour the olive oil into a heavy-bottomed soup pot or kettle of at least 6-quart capacity. Place the pot over medium heat and stir in the onions. Cook until the onions are tender and translucent but not brown, 8 to 10 minutes.

Stir in the garlic, tomatoes, and seasonings. Simmer for 3 to 4 minutes, then pour in the liquid. Salt lightly to taste and boil slowly, loosely covered, for 45 minutes to 1 hour.

Strain, pressing the juices out of the ingredients, and return the resulting liquid to the pot. Taste carefully for seasoning.

ROUILLE

"This marvelous sauce for all garlic lovers makes any fine fish soup even more splendid," says Julia. "Use it also on pasta, boiled potatoes, boiled fish, poached eggs—on anything, in fact, that would enjoy being associated with a big touch of garlic and pimiento. It is essential here that the garlic be pureed into a fine paste—the food processor and electric blender are not recommended, since they chop rather than puree." As in any dish that uses raw egg yolks, be sure the eggs you use are fresh and have been kept under refrigeration. If you make the rouille ahead, or have any left over, store it, tightly covered, in the refrigerator.

6 LARGE GARLIC CLOVES

¼ TEASPOON SALT

18 OR SO LARGE FRESH BASIL LEAVES, CHOPPED COARSE, OR 1 ½ TEASPOONS DRIED SAVORY, OREGANO, OR THYME

¾ CUP FRESH BREAD CRUMBS FROM HOMEMADE-TYPE WHITE BREAD, CRUSTS OFF, LIGHTLY PRESSED DOWN

2 TO 3 TABLESPOONS HOT SOUP BASE OR MILK

2 LARGE EGG YOLKS

⅓ CUP BOTTLED RED PIMIENTOS, DRAINED

¾ TO 1 CUP EXTRA-VIRGIN OLIVE OIL

FEW DROPS TABASCO

SALT AND FRESH-GROUND PEPPER

Mash the garlic cloves with the flat of a heavy knife, remove the peel and pound them in a mortar or heavy bowl while adding the salt. Pound to a smooth paste, and continue pounding while adding the herbs.

When well mashed and blended, pound in the bread crumbs and the soup base or milk. When the mixture has formed a paste, pound in the egg yolks, then the pimientos.

At this point, switch to a hand-held electric beater or a whisk and beat a minute or more, until very thick and sticky. Begin beating in the oil by small driblets, as though making a mayonnaise. Continue adding oil until you have a thick, hearty, heavy sauce. Season to taste with droplets of the Tabasco, and salt and pepper.

Le Brantôme (French Walnut Layer Cake)

For special occasions Julia suggests Le Brantôme: "Rather than a pound cake, a sponge cake, an angel or a lady cake, when you know they're coming, bake them this walnut cake with a whipped-cream batter, a brandy filling, chopped-nut side walls, and a white-frosted top covered with sweet words of love." It is a delicious light cake that really does taste of walnuts.

Cake

- **3** LARGE EGGS
- **1½** CUPS SUGAR
- **⅛** TEASPOON SALT
- **2** TEASPOONS PURE VANILLA EXTRACT
- **1½** CUPS UNBLEACHED ALL-PURPOSE FLOUR (MEASURE BY SCOOPING DRY-MEASURE CUPS INTO THE FLOUR AND SWEEPING OFF EXCESS)
- **2** TEASPOONS DOUBLE-ACTION BAKING POWDER
- **1** CUP (4 OUNCES) WALNUT MEATS, PULVERIZED IN AN ELECTRIC BLENDER WITH **2** TABLESPOONS SUGAR
- **1½** CUPS CHILLED WHIPPING CREAM

Break the eggs into the bowl of an electric mixer on a stand. Gradually beat in the sugar using moderate speed, then continue beating at high speed for 5 minutes or more, until the mixture is thick and the consistency of whipped cream. Beat in the salt and vanilla.

While the eggs are beating, lightly butter two cake pans about 9½ inches in diameter. Line the bottoms with wax or parchment paper and lightly butter and flour the paper. Preheat the oven to 350° F.

Place the measured flour and baking powder in a flour sifter or sieve and stir briefly. Whip the cream into Chantilly, meaning it should double in volume and hold its shape softly when a bit is lifted and dropped back onto the surface.

When the eggs are thick and creamy, sift a quarter of the flour on top, and fold it in with a rubber spatula. Plunge the spatula like a knife down into the center of the mixture, then draw it to the side of the bowl and up to surface in a rapid scoop, bringing some of the eggs up over the flour; rotate the bowl a quarter turn, and continue rapidly and gently for several scoops until the flour is almost incorporated.

Sift on, and fold in, another quarter of the remaining flour. Then scoop the whipped cream on top of the mixture, sift on more flour and a sprinkling of nuts; continue folding, alternating with sprinkles of flour and nuts until all are incorporated.

Turn the mixture into the prepared pans, dividing it as evenly as possible; the pans will be about three-quarters full. With a spatula, spread the batter evenly in the pans. Place at once in the middle level of the oven, spacing the pans diagonally from each other at far and near corners of the rack. Or, use two racks and switch the pans from one to the other halfway through baking. Bake about 25 minutes. The layers will rise to the tops of the pans, then sink lightly and brown; they are done when they show the faintest hairline of shrinkage from the sides of the pans. Let cool 10 minutes, then unmold onto racks. When the layers are cold, they may be iced, or wrapped airtight and refrigerated or frozen.

BRANDY-BUTTER FILLING:

1 LARGE EGG

3 TABLESPOONS COGNAC OR ARMAGNAC

4 TO 6 TABLESPOONS UNSALTED BUTTER

1½ TEASPOONS CORNSTARCH

1 CUP PLUS 3 TABLESPOONS SUGAR

1½ CUPS APRICOT JAM

ABOUT 1½ CUPS CHOPPED WALNUTS OR ALMONDS

Beat the egg, brandy, 2 tablespoons butter, the cornstarch, and 1 cup sugar together over moderate heat in a small saucepan and let boil, stirring, for 2 to 3 minutes to cook the starch. Remove from the heat and beat in 2 to 4 additional tablespoons of butter. The filling will thicken more as it cools.

Make an apricot glaze by sieving the apricot jam into a saucepan. Stir in the 3 tablespoons sugar and cook to the thread stage, 228° F. Keep the glaze warm while icing the cake.

Spread as much of the cool filling as you wish on top of one of the cake layers, and set it on a circular cake rack over a tray. Turn the other layer upside down on it. Using a pastry brush, paint the top and sides of the cake with the warm apricot glaze. Immediately, before the glaze has set, brush the chopped nuts around the sides of the cake. Transfer the cake to a serving dish.

(continued)

Glace Royale Frosting

1 large egg white

¼ teaspoon lemon juice

2 cups or more confectioners' sugar, sifted

1 teaspoon or so Cognac or pure vanilla extract

Optional: Melted bitter chocolate or food coloring

This is easiest to make in a small (4-cup) bowl with a hand-held electric mixer. Start beating the egg white, lemon juice, and 1 cup of confectioners' sugar, beating in more sugar until the frosting is a thick white paste. Beat in a teaspoon of flavoring, then continue beating several minutes until the frosting is thick, smooth, and stands in peaks.

You may need to beat in a little more sugar if the frosting does not thicken enough, but do not do so until you have worked the mixture several minutes and given the egg white and lemon juice time to do their job of stiffening. If you are not using the frosting immediately, or have leftovers, scoop it into a jar, lay four layers of damp paper towels on top and cover airtight.

To Finish the Cake

Spread a thin layer of frosting over the glaze on top of the cake. To make decorations or write messages, mix a little melted chocolate into an equal amount of frosting, or use drops of food coloring, and squeeze the frosting through a paper decorating cone.

AUTUMN RECIPES

Seared Sea Scallops
with Citrus-Ginger Vinaigrette

This dish from Annie Roberts is an elegant first course before roasted, baked, poached, or grilled fish. The Oriental flavors of soy sauce and ginger add just an accent, and are good with Chenin or Fumé Blanc. Fresh sea scallops are essential to sear properly; ask your fish supplier to let you know when they are available. The frizzle of fried leeks provides lovely texture and flavor; the leeks may be fried an hour or two ahead of serving and recrisped for 5 minutes in a 300° F oven.

Vinaigrette and Salad

1 ½	TABLESPOONS LIME JUICE
1 ½	TABLESPOONS CHAMPAGNE VINEGAR OR WHITE WINE VINEGAR
1 ½	TABLESPOONS SOY SAUCE
½	TABLESPOON GRATED OR MINCED GINGERROOT
½	TEASPOON LIME ZEST
1	SHALLOT, MINCED
¼	CUP PEANUT OIL
2	QUARTS MIXED BABY LETTUCE LEAVES
2	HEADS BELGIAN ENDIVE, LEAVES SEPARATED

Mix the lime juice, vinegar, soy sauce, gingerroot, lime zest, and shallot together in a small bowl. Whisk in the peanut oil to make an emulsion. Wash the lettuces and dry them; wash the Belgian endive leaves and dry them. Reserve separately. Reserve the vinaigrette.

Leeks and Scallops

1	LEEK, ABOUT 8 OUNCES
	PEANUT OR CANOLA OIL TO FRY THE LEEK
1 ½	POUNDS FRESH SEA SCALLOPS
	SALT AND FRESH-GROUND PEPPER
2	TABLESPOONS OLIVE OIL

Trim the leek to 3 or 4 inches of green. Cut the leek in half lengthwise, then in half crosswise. Julienne the leek and wash very well. Dry the leek thoroughly with several kitchen or paper towels.

Heat enough peanut oil to come ½ inch up the sides of a 9- or 10-inch sauté pan. When the oil is about 360° F, add half of the prepared leek. Stir the shreds continually until they are golden brown, about 30 seconds. Remove to paper towels to drain and fry the remaining shreds. Reserve until ready to serve, recrisping if necessary for 5 minutes in a 300° F oven.

Trim the scallops of any connective tissue. Slice them ¼ inch thick crosswise. Pat the scallops very dry, and season with salt and pepper.

Heat a large nonstick sauté pan until very hot. Add the olive oil to the pan; then add the scallops, in batches if necessary, and sear on one side to a rich golden brown, about 2 minutes. Turn the scallops onto a platter.

To Finish the Dish

Toss the lettuces and endives separately with about half of the vinaigrette. Arrange the lettuces in the center of serving plates or a platter, and arrange the endives around the lettuces. Place the scallops, seared side up, on the lettuces and drizzle with the remaining vinaigrette. Scatter the fried leek on top and serve immediately.

Smoked Duck Sausage Croutons
SERVES 4

Annie suggests that if you can't find duck sausage, use any smoked sausage without hot peppers. The Cabernet vinaigrette is so good that your family or guests may ask for more croutons; the recipe is easily doubled. The vinaigrette also works well as a brush-on marinade for chicken and beef. It's interesting to serve this appetizer with another red wine—Pinot Noir, Zinfandel, or Merlot—or even a full-bodied Chardonnay.

1 BAGUETTE

8 OUNCES SMOKED DUCK SAUSAGE

½ CUP CABERNET SAUVIGNON

¼ CUP BALSAMIC VINEGAR

1 SHALLOT, DICED FINE

1 TEASPOON DIJON-STYLE MUSTARD

⅓ CUP OLIVE OIL

SALT AND FRESH-GROUND PEPPER

2 OR 3 FRESH ITALIAN PARSLEY OR THYME SPRIGS, LEAVES CHOPPED FINE

Slice 12 pieces of the baguette about ⅓ inch thick. Toast the slices and reserve. Grill the sausage briefly or heat it through in a sauté pan. Set aside to cool.

Combine the Cabernet, vinegar, and shallot in a nonreactive saucepan. Bring the mixture to a boil and reduce to about ¼ cup. Remove from the heat and whisk in the mustard and olive oil. Season with salt and pepper.

Slice the sausage about ⅛ inch thick. Toss the sausage with the vinaigrette and let stand a few minutes.

When ready to serve, arrange the sausage slices on the croutons and sprinkle with the chopped parsley or thyme.

CHÈVRE-STUFFED RADICCHIO

These unusual appetizers from Annie Roberts are especially good served with Chardonnay. The creamy tartness of the goat cheese and the bittersweetness of the radicchio call for the balance of acidity from Chardonnay grapes and the richness the wine develops from its time in oak barrels.

> 1 LARGE HEAD RADICCHIO, ABOUT 10 OUNCES
> 11 OUNCES CHÈVRE, PREFERABLY FROM CALIFORNIA
> 2 TABLESPOONS BALSAMIC VINEGAR
> 2 TABLESPOONS SHERRY VINEGAR
> ½ CUP EXTRA-VIRGIN OLIVE OIL
> SALT AND FRESH-GROUND PEPPER
> ¼ CUP FINE-DICED SHALLOTS
> OPTIONAL: CROUTONS MADE FROM A BAGUETTE

Core the radicchio and carefully remove the leaves. Rinse and dry them in a salad spinner.

Divide the chèvre into 16 pieces and roll each piece into a ball shape. Place one ball of chèvre in a radicchio leaf. Roll the leaf around the chèvre, tucking the edges in as best you can, and secure with toothpicks. Finish rolling the cheese in the radicchio leaves and set on a baking sheet. Preheat the oven broiler.

Add the balsamic and sherry vinegars to a small bowl and whisk in the olive oil to make an emulsion. Season well with salt and pepper.

When ready to serve, brush some of the vinaigrette over the radicchio packages. Place the baking sheet 5 or 6 inches from the broiler and cook until the radicchio is browned, about 4 minutes, turning the packages with tongs two or three times.

Place the radicchio packages on a serving platter and remove the toothpicks. Drizzle with the remaining vinaigrette and sprinkle with the chopped shallots. Serve immediately, with croutons, if desired.

LATE HARVEST TOMATO AND BASIL SAUCE WITH PASTA

SERVES 3 TO 4 AS A MAIN COURSE, 6 TO 8 AS A FIRST COURSE

Robert and Margrit love pasta dishes because they were raised eating them, because pasta is easy to prepare and adaptable as a first or main course, and because pasta is good with many kinds of wine. Margrit likes to make this with the last garden tomatoes and basil in October, and in winter with canned tomatoes and dried herbs. The sauce is good with imported spaghetti or penne and fresh fettuccine or tagliarini.

- **1** ONION, DICED FINE
- **1** SHALLOT, DICED FINE
- **2** TABLESPOONS EXTRA-VIRGIN OLIVE OIL
- **2** POUNDS RIPE TOMATOES OR ONE 28-OUNCE CAN PLUM TOMATOES
- **¼** CUP DRY WHITE WINE
- **3** GARLIC CLOVES, PEELED
- **1** FRESH OREGANO SPRIG OR ½ TEASPOON DRIED OREGANO
- **2** FRESH THYME SPRIGS OR ½ TEASPOON DRIED THYME
- **4** FRESH ITALIAN PARSLEY SPRIGS
- **2** FRESH BASIL SPRIGS, LEAVES SHREDDED, OR 1 TEASPOON DRIED BASIL
- SALT AND FRESH-GROUND PEPPER
- **1** POUND DRIED PASTA OR 1 ½ POUNDS FRESH PASTA
- GARNISH: FRESH-GRATED PARMESAN CHEESE

Soften the onion and shallot in the olive oil in a nonreactive saucepan over medium-low heat. Peel, seed, and dice the fresh tomatoes, or drain the canned tomatoes and squeeze the tomatoes to rid them of most seeds. Add the tomatoes, wine, and garlic to the pan.

Tie the oregano, thyme, and parsley together to make a bouquet garni and add it to the sauce. Or, add the dried oregano, thyme, and basil along with the parsley. Cover the pan and simmer the sauce for 30 minutes. Uncover the pan and reduce the sauce if necessary while the pasta cooks.

Bring an abundant pot of water to a boil to cook the pasta. Salt it well and add the pasta. Cook until the pasta is al dente and drain.

Remove the bouquet garni (or parsley sprigs) and the garlic cloves from the sauce, and stir in the shredded basil leaves. Toss the pasta with the sauce and serve hot. Pass freshly grated Parmesan cheese.

PASSADELLE

This homey, delicious soup is fondly remembered by Robert's sister, Helen Mondavi Ventura, as "worm soup," because the slender bread-crumb dumplings looked to the children like worms as they came from Rosa Mondavi's meat grinder. For the "worm" effect, you need a meat grinder with round holes approximately ⅜ inch in diameter. Even if your grinder doesn't have round holes, or the holes have a different diameter, the dumplings will still taste good.

8 CUPS CHICKEN BROTH

2 HEAPING CUPS FINE DRY BREAD CRUMBS

1 TABLESPOON UNBLEACHED ALL-PURPOSE FLOUR

1 TEASPOON SALT

LARGE PINCH GROUND CINNAMON

LARGE PINCH FRESH-GRATED NUTMEG

1 CUP FRESH-GRATED PARMESAN CHEESE

1 LEMON, ZEST REMOVED AND 1 TEASPOON MINCED

3 LARGE EGGS

OPTIONAL GARNISH: CHOPPED FRESH PARSLEY
    LEAVES

Bring the chicken broth to a simmer in a large saucepan.

Place the bread crumbs in a mixing bowl. Add the flour, salt, cinnamon, nutmeg, cheese, and lemon zest and mix well together.

Break the eggs into the mixture, and working with your hands, combine the eggs thoroughly with the bread crumbs and cheese. Add enough juice from the lemon to form a very stiff dough.

Making sure your meat grinder is very clean, place the dough, in batches, in the grinder fitted with an attachment to make about ⅜-inch diameter dumplings. Turn the grinder slowly over a plate, cutting the passadelle about 2½ inches long.

When all the dumplings have been formed, add them to the simmering chicken broth and cook at a simmer for 10 minutes. Serve immediately in warm soup plates, garnished with parsley, if desired.

Marinated Chèvre Salad

Michael Chipchase, the Vineyard Room chef who created this recipe, says that a long marination, about a day, is preferable so the chèvre can absorb the herbal flavors. Michael likes to serve this with Chevrignon; Chardonnay is also good with it. To make the concasse, peel and seed a small yellow and a small red tomato and chop each of them very fine. Cherry tomatoes may be chopped without peeling and seeding. Depending on your menu, the salad may serve as a first course or as a salad course after the entrée.

Chèvre and Marinade

- **5 TO 6 OUNCES CHÈVRE, PREFERABLY FROM CALIFORNIA**
- **1 LARGE SHALLOT, MINCED AND RINSED IN COLD WATER**
- **1 GARLIC CLOVE, MINCED**
- **1 TABLESPOON CHOPPED FRESH CHIVES**
- **1 TABLESPOON CHOPPED FRESH CHERVIL**
- **1½ TEASPOONS CHOPPED FRESH ITALIAN PARSLEY LEAVES**
- **1½ TEASPOONS CHOPPED FRESH LEMON THYME LEAVES**
- **2 TABLESPOONS CHAMPAGNE VINEGAR OR WHITE WINE VINEGAR**
- **¼ CUP EXTRA-VIRGIN OLIVE OIL**
- **SALT AND COARSE-GROUND BLACK PEPPER**

Slice the chèvre into six portions and place in a dish just large enough to hold it in one layer. Mix the remaining ingredients together and pour over the chèvre. Marinate at least 6 hours, or up to 24 hours.

Salad and Accompaniments

- **1 SOURDOUGH BAGUETTE**
- **1 GARLIC CLOVE, PEELED AND HALVED**
- **ABOUT ¼ CUP EXTRA-VIRGIN OLIVE OIL, OR TO TASTE**
- **1 QUART MIXED BABY SALAD GREENS**
- **1 TABLESPOON BALSAMIC VINEGAR**
- **¼ CUP RED TOMATO CONCASSE (SEE NOTE ABOVE)**
- **¼ CUP YELLOW TOMATO CONCASSE (SEE NOTE ABOVE)**
- **SALT AND COARSE-GROUND BLACK PEPPER**

Preheat the oven to 350° F. Cut 12 slices from the baguette on a diagonal, each about ⅜ inch thick. Rub the bread on one side with the garlic clove and brush lightly with olive oil. Place the bread on a baking sheet and toast until golden brown, about 10 minutes.

Meanwhile, wash and dry the salad greens.

When ready to serve, dress the salad lightly with the balsamic vinegar and olive oil to taste and season lightly with salt and pepper.

Arrange the salad on plates and place a piece of marinated chèvre in the center of each salad. Spoon a little of each tomato concasse around the chèvre. Place 2 slices of garlic toast on each plate and serve immediately.

GRILLED LAMB LOIN WITH ROMESCU SAUCE

This unusual preparation of lamb from Annie Roberts combines pomegranate juice and Pinot Noir in the marinade. The lamb takes on a deep, sweet-tart and herbal flavor that is counterpointed by the peppers and almonds in the sauce. Couscous and broth-braised or steamed vegetables make fine accompaniments.

LAMB AND MARINADE

- 1 **BONELESS LAMB LOIN, WITH TENDERLOIN, ABOUT 3 POUNDS**
- ½ **CUP POMEGRANATE JUICE OR UNSWEETENED CONCENTRATE (AVAILABLE AT MIDDLE EASTERN MARKETS)**
- ¼ **CUP PINOT NOIR**
- ¼ **CUP OLIVE OIL**
- 2 **GARLIC CLOVES, CRUSHED**
- 1 **FRESH ROSEMARY SPRIG OR 1 TEASPOON DRIED ROSEMARY**

Place the lamb in a dish that just holds it. Whisk together the pomegranate juice, wine, olive oil, and garlic. Remove the leaves from the fresh rosemary sprig and bruise them by rubbing between your hands. Add them to the marinade. Or, crumble the dried rosemary into the marinade. Pour the marinade over the lamb. Marinate at cool room temperature for 2 or 3 hours, turning occasionally.

ROMESCU SAUCE

- 1 **LARGE EGG YOLK**
- 1½ **TABLESPOONS LEMON JUICE**
- ¾ **CUP OLIVE OIL**
- 2 **TEASPOONS MINCED GARLIC**
- **SALT**
- ½ **CUP GROUND ALMONDS**
- 1 **RIPE TOMATO, PEELED, SEEDED, AND DICED**
- 1 **RED BELL PEPPER, ROASTED, SEEDED, PEELED, AND DICED**
- ¼ **TEASPOON CAYENNE PEPPER, OR TO TASTE**
- 2 **TABLESPOONS RED WINE VINEGAR**
- 1 **TABLESPOON TOMATO PASTE**

Make an aioli by placing the egg yolk and lemon juice in a food processor or a blender. (Again, be sure the eggs are fresh and have been kept refrigerated, to avoid salmonella.) With the motor running, slowly drizzle in the olive oil until the mixture has emulsified. Stir in the garlic and salt to taste. Reserve the aioli.

Place the almonds, tomato, roasted pepper, cayenne pepper, vinegar, and tomato paste in a food processor. Process until the sauce is well combined, about 1 minute. Stir in the aioli and adjust the seasoning with salt, cayenne pepper, or vinegar as necessary.

TO FINISH THE LAMB

When ready to grill the lamb, prepare a medium-hot grill. Brush the rosemary from the lamb. Grill the lamb until it is rare, turning it frequently, 10 to 15 minutes. Remove to a cutting board and let stand for about 10 minutes. Salt the lamb lightly and slice it in about ¼-inch slices. Serve with the romescu sauce on the side.

MOULARD DUCK BREAST WITH CABERNET THYME SAUCE

The roasting preparation and the full-flavored wine sauce make this dish especially suited to autumn and winter. For a special dinner, serve the duck with Rice Pilaf with Currants and Toasted Pine Nuts (page 72), and either precede or follow it with Marinated Chèvre Salad (page 67). Moulard ducks are very large and have a thick layer of fat over the breast. Trim the fat from the breast before serving, if desired.

The duck takes on the best flavor if marinated overnight.

DUCK AND MARINADE

- 1 WHOLE MOULARD DUCK BREAST, OR 2 WHOLE LONG ISLAND DUCK BREASTS
- 1 SCANT TABLESPOON KOSHER SALT
- 1 TABLESPOON MINCED SHALLOTS
- 1 TABLESPOON CHOPPED FRESH ITALIAN PARSLEY LEAVES
- 1 TABLESPOON BLACK PEPPERCORNS, CRACKED
- ½ BAY LEAF, CRUMBLED
- 1 GARLIC CLOVE, MINCED
- 1 FRESH THYME SPRIG, LEAVES CHOPPED

Score the duck skin in a close crosshatch pattern, being careful not to cut into the flesh. Mix the remaining ingredients together. Rub the duck breast on both sides with the mixture. Cover and refrigerate for 6 to 24 hours.

Remove the duck from the refrigerator about an hour before serving. Make the sauce while the duck is coming to room temperature.

SAUCE

- 1 CUP CABERNET SAUVIGNON
- 2 TABLESPOONS BALSAMIC VINEGAR
- 1 GARLIC CLOVE, MINCED
- 1 SHALLOT, MINCED
- 3 FRESH THYME SPRIGS
- 5 BLACK PEPPERCORNS
- 1 SMALL RIPE TOMATO, ABOUT 6 OUNCES, SEEDED AND DICED
- 1 CUP DUCK OR CHICKEN STOCK
- 4 TABLESPOONS CHILLED UNSALTED BUTTER, CUT INTO 16 PIECES
- SALT AND FRESH-GROUND PEPPER

Combine the wine, vinegar, garlic, shallot, thyme, peppercorns, and tomato in a nonreactive saucepan and reduce the liquid by half over medium-high heat. Add the duck or chicken stock and reduce by half again. Strain the liquid into a clean saucepan and reserve.

TO FINISH THE DUCK

When ready to cook the duck, preheat the oven to 400° F. Heat a nonstick sauté pan over medium-high heat. Wipe the marinade from the duck breasts.

Sear the duck breasts skin side down until nicely browned, about 5 minutes. Place the duck breasts, skin side up, on a baking sheet and cook until rare or medium-rare, 5 to 15 minutes, depending on the kind of duck you are cooking. Remove the duck from the oven and let stand for 5 minutes while you finish the sauce.

Heat the sauce over medium-low heat. Add the butter, a few bits at a time, swirling to incorporate. Adjust the seasoning.

If desired, remove the skin from the duck before slicing. Slice the duck ¼ inch thick on a diagonal. Place on warm plates or platter and surround with the sauce. Serve immediately.

Gary Jenanyan's Braised Rabbit Tarts with Sage and Pancetta

This elegant main course is most satisfying in its complex flavors and textures. Though it may seem complicated, it can be prepared in stages. Make the rabbit stock and caramelize the onions a day ahead. Render the pancetta, sauté the mushrooms, and cook and bone the rabbit saddles and hind legs early in the day. If wild mushrooms are not in season, it is worth making the dish with brown cultivated mushrooms. Gary points out that pancetta varies in salt content. For this recipe, you will need a mildly salty pancetta. If yours is quite salty, reduce the amount by 2 ounces.

3 WHOLE FRYER RABBITS, 2½ POUNDS EACH

3 RABBIT OR 4 CHICKEN LIVERS

ABOUT 1 CUP MILK

8 CUPS CHICKEN BROTH

4 ONIONS, ABOUT 5 TO 6 OUNCES EACH, 4 HALVED AND SLICED THIN, 2 DICED

3 TABLESPOONS PEANUT OR SAFFLOWER OIL

6 OUNCES PANCETTA, SLICED THIN

12 LARGE FRESH SAGE LEAVES, CUT IN FINE SHREDS

SALT AND FRESH-GROUND PEPPER

8 OUNCES CHANTERELLE OR MOREL MUSHROOMS, OR BROWN CULTIVATED MUSHROOMS

6 TABLESPOONS UNSALTED BUTTER

6 GARLIC CLOVES, MINCED

2 LARGE CARROTS, ABOUT 5 OUNCES EACH, PEELED AND DICED

4 GARLIC CLOVES, CRUSHED

1 CUP DRY WHITE WINE

8 SMALL CARROTS, ABOUT 1½ OUNCES EACH

½ PINT CHERRY TOMATOES

½ CUP CHOPPED FRESH ITALIAN PARSLEY LEAVES

8 PREBAKED 4-INCH PUFF OR SHORT PASTRY TART SHELLS

SMALL BUNCH FRESH CHERVIL

Remove the hind legs and saddles from the rabbits, or have your butcher do this. Rinse all the rabbit pieces well, and pat dry. Preheat the oven to 450° F.

Trim the flaps from the saddles and reserve for the stock. Place the hind legs and saddles in a dish, cover well, and refrigerate until ready to use. Place the livers in a small dish and cover with milk. Place a lid or plastic wrap on the dish and refrigerate until ready to use.

With a cleaver, cut the remaining rabbit into about 3-inch pieces. Brown the pieces, in one layer in one or two shallow roasting pans, in the oven. Turn the rabbit pieces to brown all over. Total browning time is about 30 minutes.

When the rabbit is well-browned, transfer it to a large casserole and add the chicken broth. Bring the broth to a boil, lower the heat to a simmer, and skim the broth occasionally. Reduce the broth to about 2 cups; it will take about an hour. Strain the rabbit stock and reserve.

Sweat the sliced onions in the oil, covered, over low heat in a large sauté pan until they are very soft. Uncover and caramelize the onions lightly, stirring frequently.

Cook the pancetta in a small sauté pan until it is light brown and most of the fat has been rendered. Meanwhile, remove the connective tissues from the livers. Remove the pancetta and reserve. Pour off all but a tablespoon of pancetta fat from the pan and sauté the livers and sage over medium-high heat until the livers are cooked to medium rare. Remove the livers to a plate and season with salt and pepper.

Trim and clean the mushrooms. Slice about ¼ inch thick. Melt 3 tablespoons of the butter in a sauté pan over medium-high heat. Sauté the mushrooms with the minced garlic until the mushroom juices have evaporated and the mushrooms are slightly crisp, about 7 minutes. Remove the mushrooms to a plate and season with salt and pepper.

Preheat the oven to 400° F.

Melt the remaining butter in two large sauté pans over high heat. Add the rabbit saddles and hind legs and brown them well all over. Transfer the rabbit to a roasting pan and add the diced carrots and onions, the crushed garlic, white wine, and reserved rabbit stock. Cover the pan tightly with foil and bring the stock to a boil over high heat.

Immediately place the roasting pan in the oven for 15 minutes. Uncover the pan, turn the rabbit, cover the pan again, and cook in the oven for 10 minutes, until the rabbit is just done. Test for doneness by piercing a hind leg with a small sharp knife. The meat should be medium rare. Remove the saddles and cook the legs a few minutes longer, if necessary.

When the rabbit is cooked, remove it to a platter to cool. Meanwhile, make the sauce by straining the stock into a saucepan and reducing it to about 2 cups, skimming frequently. Adjust the seasoning with salt and pepper. When the rabbit is cool enough to handle, remove the meat from the bones and cut it in bite-size pieces.

When ready to finish the dish, preheat the oven to 400° F. Peel and trim the small carrots and pan-steam them in a little water until just done, about 5 minutes. Wash, stem, and cut the cherry tomatoes in half from the stem ends.

Combine the rabbit meat, livers, mushrooms, and pancetta in a large bowl. Add the parsley and adjust the seasoning.

Place the tart shells on a baking sheet lined with parchment paper. Divide the caramelized onions among the shells and mound the rabbit mixture on top. Bake the tarts for 5 to 7 minutes, enough to heat thoroughly.

Place each tart in the center of a warm plate. Moisten each with the sauce and spoon a little around the tarts. Garnish the plates with the cooked carrots, cherry tomatoes, and chervil sprigs. Serve hot.

SAUTÉED SPINACH WITH GARLIC

SERVES 4 TO 6

The hint of garlic and lemon juice in this dish gives it an interesting edge, but does not overwhelm, making the dish a good accompaniment to many main courses, and the wines served with them.

3 BUNCHES FRESH SPINACH, ABOUT 2¼ POUNDS
1 LARGE GARLIC CLOVE, PEELED AND CUT IN HALF LENGTHWISE
4 TABLESPOONS UNSALTED BUTTER
SALT AND FRESH-GROUND PEPPER TO TASTE
ABOUT 1 TEASPOON LEMON JUICE

Wash the spinach well and shake it gently to remove some water. Combine the garlic and butter in a large nonreactive pan with a lid and place over medium heat.

When the butter has melted, add the spinach. Cover the pan for 1 minute, then uncover and stir until the spinach has wilted.

Remove the pan from the heat and season with salt, pepper, and a squeeze of lemon juice. Discard the garlic clove and serve the spinach hot.

Rice Pilaf with Currants and Toasted Pine Nuts

This is the first dish that chef Gary Jenanyan learned to make from his mother, when he was nine years old. It remains a favorite of his, and not only for sentimental reasons. It is a tasty accompaniment to many main courses, serving particularly well as a counterpoint to dishes with a wine sauce. It can also be prepared early in the day and reheated before serving. If you do this, add the currants and pine nuts just before reheating the pilaf, covered, over medium-low heat for 10 minutes, stirring frequently.

6   TABLESPOONS UNSALTED BUTTER

1   TEASPOON SALT

½   TEASPOON FRESH-GROUND PEPPER

2¼   CUPS CHICKEN BROTH

1½   TABLESPOONS CANOLA, PEANUT, OR SAFFLOWER OIL

2   OUNCES CAPELLINI OR VERMICELLI, BROKEN INTO THIRDS

1   CUP LONG-GRAIN WHITE RICE

¼   CUP TOASTED PINE NUTS

¼   CUP DRIED CURRANTS, SOAKED IN WARM WATER FOR 10 MINUTES, DRAINED, AND PATTED DRY

Combine the butter, salt, pepper, and chicken broth in a saucepan, with a long handle if you have one. Bring the mixture to a simmer, uncovered.

Meanwhile, heat the oil in a 3- or 4-quart heavy-bottomed casserole over medium heat. Add the capellini and stir continually with a fork until the pasta is golden brown all over, about 5 minutes. Add the rice all at once and stir until the rice grains change color from pale white to bright pearl white, about 7 minutes.

Bring the broth mixture to a boil. Very carefully, pour the boiling chicken broth over the rice and vermicelli, holding a lid in front of the rice/pasta pan and pouring the broth in from the side. A considerable amount of steam will immediately rise from the casserole.

When the steam has subsided, scrape down the sides of the casserole to make sure all of the rice is covered with broth. Cover, reduce the heat to the barest simmer, and cook for 20 minutes. Set the lid so the pan is slightly uncovered and cook until all the broth is absorbed, 5 to 10 minutes.

Spread the pine nuts on a baking sheet and toast them in a 350° F oven, about 3 to 5 minutes.

Fold in the currants and pine nuts and fluff the rice gently, preferably with a wooden fork. Cover and let stand for 15 minutes before serving. Adjust the seasoning if necessary. Serve hot.

Apple Tart with Almond Custard

There are seemingly infinite versions of apple pies and tarts. Annie Roberts has come up with a tasty twist by adding nutty texture and flavor and a light custard. There is a distinct tartness when crème fraîche is used in the custard. You will need half of the pastry dough for this recipe; freeze the remaining portion for another tart or pie.

PASTRY DOUGH, PAGE 193

2 POUNDS FIRM COOKING APPLES, SUCH AS GRANNY SMITH OR WINESAP

4 TABLESPOONS UNSALTED BUTTER

¼ CUP DARK RUM

¼ CUP PLUS ⅓ CUP SUGAR

⅓ CUP CRÈME FRAÎCHE OR ¼ CUP WHIPPING CREAM

1 LARGE EGG, LIGHTLY BEATEN

½ CUP ALMONDS, GROUND

Divide the pastry dough in half and roll one portion to fit a 9½-inch tart pan with removable bottom; reserve the remaining portion for another use. Chill the tart shell in the freezer for at least 15 minutes. Preheat the oven to 400° F.

Line the tart shell with foil and beans or pie weights, and place it on a baking sheet. Bake for 10 minutes. Remove the foil and beans, reduce the heat to 375° F, and bake for 10 minutes longer. If the edges begin to brown too much, cover them with foil. Remove the shell to a rack to cool to room temperature. Reset the oven to 400° F.

Meanwhile, peel and core the apples and cut them into about 1-inch cubes. Combine the butter, rum, and ¼ cup sugar in a nonreactive sauté pan. Place over high heat and add the apples. Toss or stir the butter-rum mixture to coat the apples well. Cook until the apples are golden brown and slightly caramelized, 10 to 15 minutes, stirring frequently. The apples should be tender, yet still hold their shape. There will not be much liquid left. Remove the pan from the heat and let the apples cool slightly.

Combine the crème fraîche or whipping cream with the egg, almonds, and ⅓ cup sugar.

Distribute the apples in the baked tart shell. Pour the custard over the apples and bake the tart for 25 to 30 minutes, until the custard is firm in the center and the top is golden brown. Remove to a rack to cool. Serve slightly warm or at room temperature.

STEAMED PERSIMMON PUDDING

This seasonal treat is one that Margrit makes every autumn. Use the pointed variety of persimmon (*Diospyros kaki*), rather than the round flat Japanese persimmon, and be sure the persimmons are as soft as jelly. The pudding may be made the day ahead, cooled to room temperature, and refrigerated. Unmold it and wrap well in foil before reheating by steaming on a rack. The hard sauce that follows is a festive addition to the pudding, but the pudding is moist and delicious on its own.

3 VERY RIPE AND SOFT PERSIMMONS, ABOUT
  1 POUND
½ CUP (4 OUNCES) UNSALTED BUTTER, AT ROOM
  TEMPERATURE
6 TABLESPOONS LIGHT BROWN SUGAR, PACKED
6 TABLESPOONS GRANULATED SUGAR
1 LARGE EGG, BEATEN
1 CUP SIFTED UNBLEACHED ALL-PURPOSE FLOUR
1¾ TEASPOONS BAKING SODA
1 TEASPOON GROUND CINNAMON
¼ TEASPOON SALT
½ CUP MILK
1 TEASPOON PURE VANILLA EXTRACT

Remove the stems from the persimmons and puree them, including the skins, in a blender or food processor. Reserve.

Beat the butter and sugar in a large bowl until light and fluffy. Add the beaten egg to the mixture and combine well. Sift the flour with the baking soda, cinnamon, and salt, and add to the butter mixture alternately with the milk. Stir the persimmon puree and vanilla extract into the batter, combining well.

Butter a 1-quart mold generously. Pour the batter into the mold and cover tightly with a lid or foil.

Place the mold on a rack in a saucepan that is deep enough to hold the mold and has a tight-fitting lid. Add water just to the bottom of the rack. Depending on the dimensions of the pan, you may need to check the water level every 30 minutes or so while the pudding is steaming. Cover the pan. (If your pan is deep enough but doesn't have a lid, use foil to cover it.) Steam the pudding on top of the stove, or in a preheated 325° F oven, for 2½ hours.

Remove the mold from the pan and cool the pudding until the mold is just warm to the touch before unmolding. Serve lukewarm or at room temperature with the hard sauce (recipe follows).

Foamy Hard Sauce

As well as being a delicious accompaniment to Steamed Persimmon Pudding, the hard sauce is also good with pound cake and bread puddings. The sauce may be made ahead, cooled to room temperature, covered well, and stored in the refrigerator for a day or two. Reheat the sauce carefully over simmering water.

- 4 TABLESPOONS UNSALTED BUTTER
- ½ CUP SUGAR
- 2 LARGE EGG YOLKS, LIGHTLY BEATEN
- 2 TABLESPOONS PLUS 1 TEASPOON COGNAC, BRANDY, OR SHERRY
- PINCH SALT
- ½ CUP HEAVY CREAM

Beat the butter and sugar together well with an electric mixer, 5 to 8 minutes. When very light and fluffy, add the egg yolks, 2 tablespoons of the Cognac, and salt, and beat well. Transfer the mixture to the top of a double boiler.

Heat the cream in a small saucepan until it just steams; do not allow to boil. Whisk the cream into the butter mixture in a thin stream, then place the double boiler top over simmering water and whisk the sauce until it is light and fluffy, and about as thick as lightly whipped cream. Remove the pan from the heat and stir in the teaspoon of Cognac.

Place the sauce in a warm serving dish and pass separately.

Vineyard Room Chocolate Cake

When the weather cools, many people who hadn't thought about chocolate—except ice cream—for months think of rich chocolate and baking. This practically pure chocolate cake is easy enough to make for the family, and elegant enough to serve after special dinners. Chocolate and Cabernet Sauvignon pair very nicely, making this a good dessert to follow a main course you are serving with a Cabernet.

- 11 TABLESPOONS UNSALTED BUTTER
- 12 OUNCES BITTERSWEET CHOCOLATE, BROKEN OR CHOPPED IN PIECES
- ¾ CUP SUGAR
- 5 LARGE EGGS, SEPARATED
- ⅓ CUP UNBLEACHED ALL-PURPOSE FLOUR
- GARNISH: CONFECTIONERS' SUGAR
- OPTIONAL GARNISH: WHIPPED CREAM

Preheat the oven to 350° F. Use 1 tablespoon of the butter to grease a 9-inch springform pan.

Melt the remaining butter, the chocolate, and sugar in a double boiler over simmering water. Remove the mixture from the heat and cool to room temperature. Whisk in the egg yolks, one at a time. Stir in the flour.

Beat the egg whites until they hold stiff peaks. Stir one fourth of the beaten whites into the chocolate mixture. Fold the remaining whites into the batter in three batches. Spoon the batter into the prepared pan.

Bake for 45 to 50 minutes, until the cake is firm and pulls from the edges of the pan. Remove the cake to a rack to cool to room temperature in the pan.

When ready to serve, remove the sides of the springform and place the cake on a platter. Sift about 2 tablespoons of confectioners' sugar over the top of the cake. Serve with whipped cream, if desired.

IN WINTER: HEARTY, SPICY WINES

WINTER

AND THE FOOD THAT GOES WITH THEM

as it does in coastal California, people notice the change in temperature and choose food and wine that warm. Our sense of what to eat when the weather turns cold is not only a physical response, but is informed by many other facts of our life. As Tim Mondavi says, "Everyone is influenced by more than just the taste of the food and wine—by the people, the season, the emotion of the occasion, whether one feels like experimenting with something new. In winter I like hearty, spicy wines and the food that goes with them."

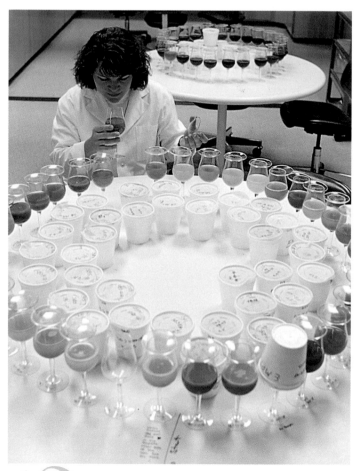

*W*inemakers work in a field that follows the seasonal cycles, which encourages a sense of ritual and repetition. The Mondavis recognize that each year is also different: In some, the grapes come to perfection in the vineyards, and the winemaker understands

how to keep this perfection. In others, the right
flavor needs to be coaxed from the grapes. Winter is the time of tasting new and old wines and
deciding when the vineyards and wines are at
the right stage for the many operations that
take place during the season. These include
pruning, grafting, and plowing; topping up
casks; racking new wine into clean barrels;
and choosing which vintages to release.

Over the years, the Mondavis return to
the foods and wines that particularly satisfy;
these are dishes, varietal wines, and vintages

that just taste good and work well, time after time. Memories, personal preferences, and chance influence this selection. Not only certain dishes, but the rituals of making and sharing them have become part of their family traditions. Dorothy Mondavi recounts the excitement of Thanksgiving Day with Tim's and her children. "In the morning we gather table decorations from the woods. Then everyone is in the kitchen: peeling, dicing, cooking, tasting, and decorating the table, until dinner comes together in a kind of hectic heaven."

The season naturally pulls us indoors, and its holidays call for taking the time to re-create cherished dishes, to celebrate our lives with friends and family. As Robert observes, "We can find those moments of harmony when we gather in good spirits, with good food and wine."

A Dinner from Rosa Mondavi

Antipasto

Cappelletti in Brodo

FUMÉ BLANC

Nonna's Roast Chicken with Dressing

Rosa Mondavi's Pastasciutta

CHARDONNAY AND CABERNET SAUVIGNON

Braised Baby Artichokes

Swiss Chard with Potatoes

The holiday menu features dishes of Rosa Mondavi, a legendary cook celebrated by everyone who tasted her food. She loved to make friends and family happy by feeding them well. She had the genius of great cooks: She set an ample, even abundant table, but the food was so well balanced that people left the table feeling perfectly satisfied, not a whit too full. Robert remembers this same quality in a meal he had at La Pyramide when Fernand Point, the extraordinary French chef, was in the kitchen. "Fernand kept sending course after course. Though I had eaten a large, late breakfast, the food he prepared was so light and balanced that I ate and enjoyed everything, without any feeling of overindulgence."

"My mother's cooking is the standard by which I measure all food."
—ROBERT MONDAVI

Rosa made exceptionally fine pasta, and would prepare several kinds during the holidays. One of her granddaughters, Serena Ventura Chickering, remembers that the kitchen would be filled with pasta in various stages of drying or resting. As Serena describes Rosa, "She was a gifted and talented cook, whose love was people. She loved to share her culinary perfections with anyone who appreciated the art of fine home cooking in a warm and genuine atmosphere. She learned to cook very young in Italy, where recipes were in the cook's head and hands, rather than in books. I loved to watch her work with her beauti-

ful, strong, and skillful hands. I would say she added warmth, charm, and love to every dish she made."

Before dinner, antipasto and bread were ready for nibbling. When the family gathered at table, Rosa brought a tureen of homemade chicken broth, in which floated toothsome cappelletti. As Tim Mondavi recalls, "The dining table would be filled with Nonna's delicious dishes: pastasciutta, which is what she called her handmade fettuccine noodles dressed with homemade tomato sauce, and roast chicken with dressing, which was everyone's favorite." Side dishes could be baby artichokes, spinach sautéed with garlic, or a salad/side dish of Swiss chard and potatoes. There was no fixed dessert, as Helen Mondavi Ventura remembers. "Mother could bake anything, and usually made what we children were fond of at the time. Some years it was a lemon chiffon pie that we all loved, or she would bake an apple cake or a crostata, a kind of Italian tart with homemade jam or jelly."

ine to accompany the food would vary according what varieties and vintages were of particular interest at that time. Tim describes the family's philosophy of pairing food and wine: "The purpose of wine is to add a dimension of pleasure. So, drink what you like and like what you drink. With most menus, it's best to start with the light, bright wines and move to the more complex, which usually means whites to reds. A fresh, sparkling wine is usually a good beginning, as it wakes up the appetite. With Nonna's cappelletti in brodo, a Fumé Blanc is excellent, as it is bright and fresh and doesn't overwhelm the delicate broth. For the roast chicken, many wines would be good: a rich, complex Chardonnay Reserve, or a Pinot Noir, or a Zinfandel or Cabernet Sauvignon, if you like them."

ANTIPASTO

MAKES ABOUT 2 QUARTS

In the 1950s Giulia Santi and her family came to the Napa Valley from the same town in Italy as the Mondavi family. Giulia spent many pleasant hours in the kitchen with Rosa Mondavi, including some making this pickled vegetable antipasto. The vegetables were always cooked separately so that each would be crisp-tender and succulent. Rosa had several variations, sometimes adding best-quality canned albacore or tuna, green or black olives, or a little tomato paste. If you wish to add tuna, use a well-drained 6-ounce can of tuna for each quart jar; you will have a few extra vegetables, which may be refrigerated and eaten within 2 or 3 days. The antipasto makes a colorful, attractive platter; you can garnish the platter with imported black and green olives and thin slices of prosciutto or salami. To trim the onions easily, start with the root end. As with any pickling, have your jars and lids sterilized (boiled at least 5 minutes) and hot when you are ready to pack the jars.

1   SMALL HEAD CAULIFLOWER, ABOUT 1 POUND

2   CARROTS

2   LARGE CELERY STALKS

2   LARGE RED BELL PEPPERS

4   CUPS WHITE WINE VINEGAR

4   CUPS WATER

2   TABLESPOONS SUGAR

16   BOILING ONIONS OR ITALIAN PICKLING ONIONS

16   BABY ARTICHOKES, ABOUT GOLF-BALL SIZE

1   LEMON, HALVED

1   TABLESPOON KOSHER SALT

¼   TEASPOON PEPPERCORNS

½   CUP OLIVE OIL

Trim the cauliflower to small florets, about 1 inch in diameter. You should have about 2 cups. Peel the carrots and cut them on a diagonal or into rounds or sticks, no larger than ½ inch thick. Trim the celery and string it. Cut into about 1-inch pieces on a diagonal. Stem and seed the bell peppers, and peel them if desired. Cut into strips about 1 inch wide and 2 inches long.

Bring a saucepan of plain water to boil to blanch the onions. Meanwhile, combine 3 cups of the vinegar with 2 cups of water and the sugar in a 4-quart or larger nonreactive pan and bring to a simmer. Keep at a bare simmer, covered, while you prepare the rest of the vegetables.

Blanch the onions for 2 minutes, refresh under cold water and drain. Peel the onions and trim the ends. Trim the artichokes to where the leaves begin to pale. Trim the

Seasons of the Vineyard
86

stem, removing any dark green or brown, rubbing with a cut lemon as you trim. Cut the tips; the artichokes will be about 1 inch in diameter.

Blanch the vegetables separately in the vinegar water, covered, at a boil in the following order: artichokes for 7 minutes; cauliflower for 5 minutes; celery for 3 minutes; onions for 4 minutes; carrots for 5 minutes; bell pepper for 2 minutes (peeled 1 minute). Remove each vegetable as it is parcooked with a skimmer-strainer or slotted spoon to a colander.

When all the vegetables have been parcooked, drain the cooking liquid. Bring the remaining vinegar, remaining water, the salt, peppercorns, and olive oil to a boil. Reduce the heat and simmer for 5 minutes.

Meanwhile, using tongs, pack the vegetables in hot, sterilized quart or pint canning jars. If you are using tuna, place it in the bottom of the jars. Divide the pickling liquid among the jars. Close with hot, sterilized canning lids and rings. The pickles may be used immediately, but are best after they have stood for a week. Store in a cool dark place up to 6 months. Store in the refrigerator after opening, and use within a week.

Cappelletti in Brodo

Marcie Mondavi Borger makes her grandmother Rosa's cappelletti every Christmas, with the help of one of her children. For Marcie, as for others in the family, re-creating and enjoying well-loved dishes such as this is a complex experience, bringing memory, and a sense of continuity and well-being, to the acts of cooking and eating. Cutting and filling the cappelletti takes some time, but they may be completely assembled a day ahead, covered loosely with plastic wrap, and refrigerated until ready to use. Or, they may be frozen individually on baking sheets, then packed in freezer bags or plastic containers and frozen for up to a month. There is usually a little leftover filling, which goes well in poultry stuffings and pasta sauces. Ground chicken may be substituted for the ground veal.

Filling

- 8 OUNCES GROUND LEAN BEEF
- 8 OUNCES GROUND PORK
- 8 OUNCES GROUND VEAL
- 2 TABLESPOONS OLIVE OIL
- ½ CUP FRESHLY GRATED PARMESAN CHEESE
- ½ CUP FRESHLY GRATED ROMANO CHEESE
- ½ CUP CHOPPED FRESH PARSLEY
- ABOUT 2 TEASPOONS GRATED LEMON ZEST
- LARGE PINCH FRESH-GRATED NUTMEG
- 2 LARGE EGGS
- SALT AND FRESH-GROUND PEPPER

If you have a meat grinder, grind the meats together. If not, mix them very well with your hands. Heat the olive oil over medium heat and add the ground meat. Cook until the meat is just cooked through, about 5 minutes, stirring frequently to make sure the meat is in small crumbs.

With a slotted spoon, remove the meat to a bowl to cool to room temperature. When the meat is cool, add the cheese, parsley, 1 teaspoon lemon zest, nutmeg, and eggs. Season well with salt and pepper, then work the mixture well together with your hands. Adjust the seasoning with lemon zest, nutmeg, or salt and pepper according to taste.

Pasta

- 3 CUPS ALL-PURPOSE UNBLEACHED FLOUR
- 5 LARGE EGGS
- 1 TABLESPOON OLIVE OIL
- ABOUT 1 TABLESPOON WATER

To make the dough by hand: Place the flour in a mixing bowl or on a work surface and make a well in it large enough to hold the eggs, olive oil, and water. Break the eggs into the well. Add the olive oil and 2 tablespoons of water. Beat the mixture lightly with a fork. Still working with the fork, incorporate flour from the bottom of the well until the dough is too stiff to work with the fork. Knead until the dough is smooth, about 5 minutes. It should be quite soft and pliable.

Divide the dough into four portions and cover it with plastic wrap or an overturned bowl. Let rest for at least 15 minutes.

To make the dough in a food processor: Place the flour in the workbowl fitted with the steel blade and pulse. Add the eggs and olive oil and process about 30 seconds. The dough should just turn over itself at the top of the bowl. If the dough is dry and does not hold together, sprinkle in a little water.

Turn the dough onto a work surface and knead it briefly. Divide the dough into four portions with a knife. Cover and let rest for at least 30 minutes before rolling.

To Assemble the Dish

4 to 5 quarts chicken broth

Salt and fresh-ground pepper

When ready to make the cappelletti, roll the pasta through a hand-cranked pasta machine as described below, or with a rolling pin if you are adept at rolling pasta very thin.

If the dough feels quite moist, flour it before putting it through the pasta machine. Begin working one portion of the dough through the machine at the widest setting of the rollers. Keep the remaining dough covered.

If the dough is still moist and soft, flour it, fold it, and run it through the widest setting another time or two. Otherwise, proceed by advancing the setting and running the dough through each setting once, unfolded, until the pasta is a little less than a millimeter thick, the last setting on some pasta machines, the next to the last on others.

Cut the rolled dough into circles about 2½-inches in diameter with a round cookie or biscuit cutter.

Place about ½ teaspoon of filling on the lower half of a pasta circle. Fold the dough over the filling, pressing the edges well and being sure to press out all the air. Gently stretch the ends of the filled pasta around to meet and press together well.

Place the cappelletti on baking sheets lined with baking parchment and sprinkled with semolina or dusted with flour. Or, place on tea towels lightly dusted with flour. Continue until the dough and filling have been used.

Let the cappelletti stand for about an hour before cooking; if you refrigerate them, turn them over after about 30 minutes so the bottoms do not become soggy. Or, freeze them.

To cook the cappelletti, bring the broth to a boil. Be sure it is well seasoned. Add

(continued)

the cappelletti and cook them at a gentle boil, for 2 to 6 minutes. When the pasta has changed from a butter to a cream color, try one to see if it is al dente.

Transfer the cappelletti and broth to a warm tureen or soup plates. Serve immediately.

ROSA MONDAVI'S PASTASCIUTTA

SERVES 8 TO 10 AS A FIRST OR SIDE COURSE

Home-canned tomato sauce, which Rosa called "conserva," brings the flavors of summer-ripe tomatoes to the seasons when they are not available. Rosa had a large repertoire of lightly sauced pasta dishes; depending on what else she was serving, she would use a little conserva with clams, anchovies, tuna, or bits of leftover meat or chicken.

1   RECIPE PASTA DOUGH (PAGE 88)

4   TABLESPOONS OLIVE OIL

3   GARLIC CLOVES, LIGHTLY SMASHED

2   CUPS ROSA MONDAVI'S TOMATO CONSERVA (PAGE 215)

½   CUP CHICKEN BROTH

3   TABLESPOONS CHOPPED FRESH ITALIAN PARSLEY

SALT AND FRESH-GROUND PEPPER

FRESH-GRATED PARMESAN CHEESE

After dividing and resting the pasta dough, roll it about ¹⁄₁₆ inch thick. Cut it into fettuccine noodles about 8 inches long. Lay the pasta on a work surface, making sure it does not stick together by dusting with a little semolina flour. Or, hang the pasta to dry slightly if you have racks, chair backs, or some other system to hang pasta.

Bring a large pot of water to a boil. Meanwhile, heat the olive oil over moderate heat in a large skillet or sauté pan. Add the garlic and heat until it is golden and has perfumed the oil. Remove the garlic. Add the tomato conserva and chicken broth and cook at a gentle simmer while you cook the pasta.

Salt the boiling water well and add the pasta. Cook until the pasta is al dente, from 1 to 5 minutes, depending on how long the pasta has been drying. Drain, reserving about ¼ cup of the cooking water.

Toss the pasta, cooking water, and parsley with the sauce. Adjust the seasoning and serve immediately. Pass the Parmesan to garnish.

Nonna's Roast Chicken with Dressing

Rosa's grandchildren called her Nonna, Italian for grandmother, and this family heirloom recipe, a favorite of hers, could well become a favorite in many family kitchens. It pleases the palates of all ages, and is handsome and ample enough to serve at family gatherings. Isabel Mondavi, Michael Mondavi's wife, re-created the dish so well that Robert Mondavi said it tasted just like his mother's. This version is from Karen Mitchell of the Model Bakery in St. Helena, who has helped Isabel prepare the chicken on some occasions.

1   7- TO 8-POUND ROASTING CHICKEN

SALT AND FRESH-GROUND PEPPER

2   CHICKEN LIVERS, ABOUT 3 OUNCES

1   CHICKEN GIZZARD, TRIMMED OF MEMBRANE

1   CHICKEN HEART

2   OUNCES SALT PORK, DICED

3   TABLESPOONS CHILLED UNSALTED BUTTER

1   SMALL GARLIC CLOVE

1 ½   CUPS FRESH BREAD CRUMBS

½   CUP FRESH-GRATED PARMESAN CHEESE

LARGE PINCH FRESH-GRATED NUTMEG

GRATED ZEST OF 1 SMALL LEMON

8   TO 10 FRESH ITALIAN PARSLEY SPRIGS, LEAVES CHOPPED FINE

½   CUP MILK

2   LARGE EGGS

Rinse the chicken well and pat dry. Season inside and out with salt and pepper. Preheat the oven to 400° F.

For the dressing, grind the chicken livers, gizzard, heart, diced salt pork, butter, and garlic clove in a meat grinder fitted with the fine blade. If you don't have a meat grinder, place the ingredients on a cutting board and chop very fine with a large knife or mezzaluna.

Place the ground ingredients in a bowl and add the bread crumbs, cheese, nutmeg, lemon zest, parsley, milk, and eggs. Combine the mixture well, seasoning well with salt and pepper.

Place the dressing in the chicken cavity and set the chicken on a rack in a roasting pan. Roast the chicken for an hour. Reduce the heat to 350° F and roast another 1 to 1½ hours, covering the chicken loosely with foil if it browns too much.

(continued)

When the juices run clear after the thigh joint is pierced with a knife, remove the chicken to a cutting board. Let it stand for about 15 minutes. Carve one side of the chicken into serving pieces and place on a platter.

On the side you have carved, detach the rib cage to expose the dressing. Remove the dressing carefully, as it will still be hot. Let it stand while you carve the rest of the chicken. Slice the dressing into serving pieces about ½ inch thick. Arrange the dressing on the platter with the chicken and serve.

BRAISED BABY ARTICHOKES   SERVES 8 TO 10

Marcia Mondavi Borger remembers these delicious baby artichokes made with both a small amount of bread crumbs and just parsley and garlic. The recipe is easily halved if you are serving fewer people. Baby artichokes take about half as long to trim as the large ones do, since the chokes don't need to be removed.

  3 LEMONS

  4 POUNDS BABY ARTICHOKES, ABOUT THE SIZE OF GOLF BALLS

¼ CUP FINE DRY BREAD CRUMBS

  4 LARGE GARLIC CLOVES, MINCED

10 TO 12 FRESH ITALIAN PARSLEY SPRIGS, LEAVES CHOPPED FINE

  4 TABLESPOONS EXTRA-VIRGIN OLIVE OIL

SALT AND FRESH-GROUND PEPPER

ABOUT ½ CUP WATER

Squeeze one lemon into a bowl of cold water; cut another in half to keep the artichokes from oxidizing and turning dark.

Trim the artichokes to the pale inner leaves. Cut about ½ inch from the tops and trim the bottoms of any dark green. Use the cut lemon as you trim, rubbing the artichokes well. As you finish each artichoke, drop it in the bowl with the lemon water. The artichokes will hold in the lemon water without too much discoloring for about an hour.

Mix the bread crumbs with the garlic, parsley, and 2 tablespoons of the olive oil. Season the mixture well with salt and pepper. Stuff a pinch of the mixture between some of the artichoke leaves close to the center of the artichokes, pulling the leaves back gently to stuff them.

Heat the remaining 2 tablespoons oil in a large nonreactive sauté pan over medium heat. Add the artichokes and cook for 2 or 3 minutes, turning them gently. Add about

½ cup water, and the juice of the remaining lemon. Season lightly with salt and pepper. Reduce the heat to low and cover the pan.

Cook until the artichokes are tender, about 15 minutes, stirring from time to time and adding a little water if necessary to keep the artichokes from sticking. Serve hot or at room temperature.

Swiss Chard with Potatoes

SERVES 8 TO 10

The combination of Swiss chard and potatoes is a very Italian one, embellished in several ways in regional Italian cooking—with Fontina and/or Parmesan cheese, with butter, with onions. This version of Rosa's can be used as a side dish, or with the addition of a little vinegar, as a salad.

4 OUNCES PANCETTA, SLICED THIN

5 TABLESPOONS OLIVE OIL

3 GARLIC CLOVES, SMASHED LIGHTLY

2 POUNDS RED OR WHITE POTATOES

3 POUNDS SWISS CHARD

SALT AND FRESH-GROUND PEPPER

OPTIONAL: ABOUT 1 TABLESPOON WINE VINEGAR

Dice the pancetta and render it over low heat until it is crisp and the fat has melted. Place the pancetta on paper towels to drain. Pour off all but a tablespoon of fat from the pan. Add the olive oil and garlic to the pan and reserve.

Scrub the potatoes well and cut them in half. Cook them in lightly salted water until they are just done, about 15 minutes. Drain, then peel the potatoes while they are still warm, if desired.

Trim and clean the chard and separate the stems and leaves. Cut the stems in about 1-inch pieces. Cut the leaves crosswise into about 1-inch shreds.

Cook the stems in lightly salted boiling water for about 3 minutes, until they are just crisp-tender. Add the leaves and cook for about 1½ minutes longer, until the chard is just cooked through. Drain the chard well and transfer it to a serving dish large enough to hold it and the potatoes.

Cut the potatoes into bite-size pieces and add them to the chard. Heat the reserved oil and garlic over low heat until the garlic is golden. Discard the garlic and toss the oil with the pancetta, chard, and potatoes. Season the vegetables well with salt and pepper. Add a little wine vinegar, if desired, and toss well. Serve warm.

Holiday Baking with the Children

Holiday Cupcakes

Kolakis

Decorated Sugar Cookies

With most members of the family working, holiday baking is less extensive than Margrit remembers when her children were young. "The fun of baking has always been centered around the children. It is a great part of family life to be with them in the kitchen, and to see what they create, which can be truly amazing. When my children were small, I would begin baking cookies in September for the holidays, and freeze them. One year I noticed, sometime in October, that Annie and Phoebe were not eating dinner. I found that they had discovered the frozen cookies, and would treat themselves all afternoon!"

Now, Phoebe Biever Holbrook, Margrit's younger daughter, carries on the tradition with her young children and their friends, making cookies and cupcakes that are simple to make, and most important, a lot of fun to decorate.

These are an adaptation of a recipe on a chocolate chip package that Margrit's daughter Phoebe makes with her children and their friends every year. The children are naturally happy to serve them to the family, and have perhaps even more fun decorating them than eating them. To make snowballs, roll the frosted cupcakes in shredded coconut. Little Christmas trees of rosemary sprigs can be sprinkled with Christmas sprinkles. Snowmen and -women can be made of miniature marshmallows on toothpicks, or by gluing the marshmallows together with frosting. Red and green paste food coloring mixed with frosting can be used to paint faces, buttons, etc., using toothpicks. Red and green licorice whips can be placed around the tops of frosted cupcakes for a wreath effect.

CUPCAKES

2½ CUPS UNBLEACHED ALL-PURPOSE FLOUR

2¼ TEASPOONS BAKING POWDER

½ TEASPOON SALT

1 CUP (8 OUNCES) UNSALTED BUTTER, AT ROOM TEMPERATURE

1½ CUPS SUGAR

2 TEASPOONS PURE VANILLA EXTRACT

4 LARGE EGGS

1½ CUPS MILK

1 PACKAGE (12-OUNCES) MINI-CHOCOLATE CHIPS, DIVIDED IN HALF

Sift together the flour, baking powder, and salt and reserve. Preheat the oven to 375° F.

Beat the butter with the sugar in a large bowl with an electric mixer. Add the vanilla and the eggs, one at a time, and beat until the mixture is smooth. Add the milk alternately with the flour mixture in three batches, combining well with a rubber spatula or wooden spoon. Stir in one portion of the chocolate chips. Do not overmix.

Place paper baking cups in muffin tins. Spoon the batter into the baking cups, filling them about three-quarters full.

Bake the cupcakes on the middle shelf of the oven for 20 to 25 minutes, until firm and springy and no batter clings to a toothpick inserted in the center of a cupcake. Remove the baking cups to a rack to cool.

FROSTING AND DECORATIONS

REMAINING PORTION OF CHOCOLATE CHIPS

½ **CUP (4 OUNCES) UNSALTED BUTTER**

2½ **CUPS CONFECTIONERS' SUGAR, SIFTED**

ABOUT ½ CUP MILK

1 **TABLESPOON LIGHT KARO SYRUP**

MINIATURE MARSHMALLOWS

TINY CANDY CANES

CHRISTMAS SPRINKLES

MINI M&Ms

RED AND GREEN LICORICE WHIPS

FRESH ROSEMARY SPRIGS

SHREDDED COCONUT

RED AND GREEN PASTE FOOD COLORING

Melt the chocolate chips in a heavy-bottomed saucepan over low heat. Off the heat, stir in the butter to make a smooth mixture.

Transfer the chocolate mixture to a bowl. Add the confectioners' sugar about ½ cup at a time, stirring well to make a smooth mixture. When the frosting seems stiff, add a tablespoon of milk to bring it to spreading consistency. Continue adding confectioners' sugar, and milk as necessary, until the frosting is smooth and spreadable. Stir in the Karo syrup.

Frost the cupcakes and decorate as desired.

KOLAKIS

Margrit learned to make these not-too-sweet cookies from her mother, and made them during all the holidays her children were growing up. Adults like them as well as children do, and they freeze well, an important holiday cookie attribute.

6 OUNCES CREAM CHEESE, AT ROOM TEMPERATURE

1 CUP (8 OUNCES) UNSALTED BUTTER, AT ROOM TEMPERATURE

2 CUPS UNBLEACHED ALL-PURPOSE FLOUR

½ TEASPOON BAKING POWDER

PINCH SALT

½ CUP RASPBERRY JAM

½ CUP APRICOT JAM

Beat the cream cheese and butter together with an electric mixer until well combined and fluffy, about 1 minute on low speed. Scrape the bowl once. Mix the flour with the baking powder and salt. Add the flour mixture in four batches, beating until most has been combined with the cream cheese and butter mixture.

Turn the dough out and knead to a smooth consistency, about 3 minutes. Divide the dough in half. Place each portion of dough between sheets of wax paper or plastic and roll out with a rolling pin about ¼ inch thick. Refrigerate the dough for about 15 minutes.

Preheat the oven to 350° F.

Cut the dough out with cookie cutters. Place the cookies on baking sheets about 1 inch apart. Indent the centers of the cookies with your finger or thumb, then fill the indentations with a heaping teaspoon of jam. Gather and reroll the extra dough, cut, and fill.

Bake the cookies in the preheated oven for 20 to 25 minutes, until pale golden on top and the edges begin to brown. Transfer to a rack to cool. Store in airtight containers for 3 to 4 days, or freeze on baking sheets, then pack in freezer bags and keep in the freezer for up to a month. To thaw the cookies, place them in one layer on serving platters until they are at room temperature.

DECORATED SUGAR COOKIES

MAKES ABOUT 3 DOZEN COOKIES

These are another of Phoebe's holiday decorating traditions, a little less flamboyant than the cupcakes. Especially for children, the more kinds of cookie cutters—reindeer and angels as well as trees and snowmen—the better, but even rounds can be decorated to represent Christmas ornaments. The dough is easy to work, making this a good cookie any time of year that you want to make cut-outs.

2 CUPS UNBLEACHED ALL-PURPOSE FLOUR

¼ TEASPOON SALT

¾ CUP (6 OUNCES) UNSALTED BUTTER, AT ROOM TEMPERATURE

¾ CUP SUGAR

1 LARGE EGG

1 TEASPOON PURE VANILLA EXTRACT

FOR DECORATION: DRAGÉES, NONPAREILS, SPRINKLES, OR COLORED SUGAR

Mix the flour and salt in a bowl. Beat the butter and sugar in a bowl with an electric mixer until fluffy, stopping to scrape down the bowl periodically. Add the egg and vanilla and beat the mixture until smooth. Add the flour mixture and beat on low speed until the dough comes together, about 2 minutes.

Turn the dough out, divide it into two portions and knead each briefly. Roll, decorate, and bake cookies at this point, or wrap the dough well in plastic wrap and refrigerate for up to 2 days, or freeze for up to 10 days. If the dough is refrigerated or frozen, allow it to come to cool room temperature before rolling.

Place each batch of dough between sheets of wax paper and roll out with a rolling pin about ¼ inch thick. Place the rolled-out dough, still in the wax paper, on baking sheets. Refrigerate for about 15 minutes, until it has stiffened slightly.

Preheat the oven to 375° F.

Cut out and decorate one piece of dough at a time. Choose the smoothest side of the dough to cut. Remove the wax paper from the side that will be down and replace it loosely. Remove the top piece of wax paper. Using any cookie cutters, cut out the dough. Transfer the cookies with a spatula to baking sheets, spacing about 1 inch apart. If you are using different-size cutters, group the cookies on the baking sheets according to size.

Decorate the cookies with dragées, nonpareils, sprinkles, or colored sugar. Gather the dough scraps to reroll and decorate while the first cookies are baking.

Bake the cookies for 10 to 12 minutes, changing rack positions halfway through, until the cookies are lightly colored and just beginning to brown around the edges.

Transfer the cookies with a spatula to racks to cool. Store in airtight containers for up to a week, or freeze on baking sheets, then pack in freezer bags and keep in the freezer for up to a month.

Classical Concert Lunch

Smoked Salmon Crepes

MÉTHODE CHAMPENOISE SPARKLING WINE

Dungeness Crab Cakes
with Jalapeño Mayonnaise

WHITE ZINFANDEL

Filet of Beef with Cabernet Sauvignon
Sauce and Arugula Butter

CABERNET SAUVIGNON

Pear Hazelnut Custard

JOHANNISBERG RIESLING

The classical concerts at the winery are held during the winter months. When Annie Roberts thinks about the menus for the Vineyard Room, whether they are public events, like the concerts, or private parties, she is always attuned to the seasons. Winter in the Napa Valley is cool and often rainy, but temperatures seldom drop much below freezing. In the winter months, Annie chooses a menu such as this one. It begins with a light appetizer for the reception, with sparkling wine. The first course features a seasonal ingredient, Dungeness crab, and is served with a salad; many kinds of lettuce are available all winter from northern California's mild coastal areas. The filet of beef, while having the depth of flavor that goes well with the Cabernet Sauvignon and in the season, is a lean cut. Desserts with fruit are one of Annie's specialties. For this one, she finds the best winter-variety pears, such as Anjou, Winter Nelis, or Winter Bartlett.

If the weather is unseasonably warm, Annie will vary the menu, perhaps poaching salmon and serving it with a Pinot Noir sauce, rather than roasting beef. She is helped in such menu changes by having an herb garden just behind the Vineyard Room. All the perennial culinary herbs thrive year-round, and the annuals in their seasons. Arugula is a winter herb in the Napa Valley, as the summers are too hot for exten-

sive cultivation. The garden is a simple classical kitchen garden in raised

beds, containing edible and cutting flowers among the herbs.

The concerts are part of the Mondavi vision that civilized life

includes all the arts and the arts enhance one another, as well as our

lives. To reflect this vision, the winery exhibits art and sculpture in the

indoor and outdoor spaces; sponsors classical, popular, and jazz con-

certs throughout the year; and hosts poetry readings.

These concerts are benefits for local projects and draw a largely local

audience.

Smoked Salmon Crepes

These crepes from Annie Roberts are good with méthode champenoise sparkling wines. If you prefer a still wine, Chardonnay would be a good match. Prepare the batter at least 30 minutes before cooking the crepes; it may be prepared up to 2 hours before cooking. Always stir the batter before pouring it into the crepe pan. If you don't have a seasoned crepe pan, a small (6- or 7-inch) nonstick pan will work. The crepes may be made ahead of time, cooled to room temperature on a plate, then covered with plastic wrap and refrigerated for a day or two, or well-wrapped and frozen for up to a month. To reheat the crepes, place them on a baking sheet in layers of four or five, cover tightly with foil, and place in a preheated 300° F oven for 10 minutes. The appetizers may be assembled an hour or two before serving.

Crepe batter

- 1 CUP UNBLEACHED ALL-PURPOSE FLOUR
- ¼ TEASPOON SALT
- 3 LARGE EGGS
- 1 CUP MILK
- ½ CUP WATER
- 4 TABLESPOONS UNSALTED BUTTER, MELTED AND COOLED

Sift the flour and salt together into a mixing bowl. Whisk the eggs, one at a time, into the center of the flour. When the mixture is fairly smooth, begin adding the milk to the center of the bowl in a stream, whisking continually.

Incorporate more of the flour from the edges of the bowl as you whisk. When the flour has all been incorporated and the mixture is smooth, whisk in the water and 3 tablespoons of the melted butter. Let the batter stand 30 minutes or longer before cooking the crepes.

When ready to cook the crepes, heat a crepe pan or small nonstick sauté pan over medium-high heat. Rub it with a paper towel dipped lightly in the remaining melted butter.

Reduce the heat to medium and pour in about 3 tablespoons of batter. Tip the pan and swirl the batter to distribute it evenly. The batter should sizzle slightly as it is added to the pan.

Cook the crepe for about 30 seconds, until the edges begin to dry and the bottom is lightly browned. Turn the crepe and cook for about 20 seconds, until lightly browned. Place the cooked crepes on a baking sheet. Continue making the crepes, removing the pan from the heat for 2 or 3 seconds before cooking the next crepe. Stir the batter frequently.

(continued)

You may need to adjust the heat and/or the amount of batter. The pan heats up during the cooking; lower the heat if necessary. Add a little more batter if your pan is large, or if you like a slightly thicker crepe.

FILLING AND ASSEMBLY

⅓ CUP SOUR CREAM

ABOUT 1 TABLESPOON MILK

6 OUNCES SMOKED SALMON, SLICED VERY THIN

SALT AND FRESH-GROUND PEPPER

JUICE OF 1 LEMON

½ BUNCH FRESH CHIVES, CUT FINE

Place the sour cream in a small dish and thin it with milk. Spread a cooled crepe with about a teaspoon of the mixture. Arrange salmon slices on half of the crepe. Season the salmon lightly with salt and pepper, and sprinkle with a few drops of lemon juice. Sprinkle a few chives over the salmon.

Roll the crepe and place it seam side down on a cutting board. Continue filling and rolling the crepes. If you are making the crepes ahead, refrigerate them until ready to serve.

When ready to serve, cut the crepes into thirds on a diagonal, or in slices, as you prefer. Arrange the crepes on a platter and sprinkle with additional chives.

DUNGENESS CRAB CAKES
WITH JALAPEÑO MAYONNAISE

SERVES 6

For incomparably fresh flavor, be sure that your fishmonger has just steamed the crab, or steam the crab yourself the morning of the day you are serving the crab cakes. Four pounds of crab in the shell yields about 1¼ pounds of crabmeat. Crab cakes are delicate to handle; take care in turning them while they are cooking.

1¼ POUNDS DUNGENESS CRABMEAT

1 CUP FRESH BREAD CRUMBS

1 LARGE EGG

JALAPEÑO MAYONNAISE (PAGE 156)

1 SHALLOT, MINCED

1½ TABLESPOONS CHOPPED FRESH ITALIAN PARSLEY LEAVES

SALT AND FRESH-GROUND PEPPER

2 TABLESPOONS CANOLA OR OTHER VEGETABLE OIL

1 SMALL HEAD RED LEAF LETTUCE, TRIMMED AND CLEANED

1 SMALL HEAD GREEN LEAF LETTUCE, TRIMMED AND CLEANED

ABOUT 1 TABLESPOON EXTRA-VIRGIN OLIVE OIL

ABOUT 1½ TEASPOONS BALSAMIC VINEGAR

Remove the cartilage from the crab, keeping the meat in as large pieces as possible. Place the crab in a bowl with the bread crumbs and toss gently together.

In another bowl, beat the egg lightly and stir in 3 tablespoons of the mayonnaise, the shallot, and the parsley. Season well with salt and pepper.

Toss the egg mixture with the crab and bread crumbs; then shape the mixture into 12 small crab cakes. Place the crab cakes on a platter lined with wax paper. Cover with wax paper and refrigerate for 1 hour, or up to 4 hours.

When ready to cook the crab cakes, heat the canola oil in a nonstick skillet or sauté pan large enough to hold the crab cakes without crowding. Or, use 2 smaller skillets. When the oil is hot, add the crab cakes and cook for 4 to 6 minutes until the cakes are golden brown, turning them once. Remove the pan from the heat.

Toss the lettuces with the olive oil and vinegar to taste. Season lightly with salt and pepper.

To serve, place the crab cakes on serving plates. Place about a tablespoon of mayonnaise next to each serving, and garnish the plates with the salad.

FILET OF BEEF WITH CABERNET SAUVIGNON SAUCE AND ARUGULA BUTTER

Pepper and thyme, which coat the beef, complement Cabernet Sauvignon particularly well. Annie Roberts usually serves the salad with the first course, since there are herb and tart flavors that keep the palate refreshed in the sauce and arugula butter. Boiled or roasted new potatoes are a nice earthy side dish with the filet.

FILET

2¼ POUNDS FILET OF BEEF
2 TABLESPOONS OLIVE OIL
2 TABLESPOONS CRUSHED BLACK PEPPER
2 TABLESPOONS CHOPPED FRESH THYME LEAVES

Trim the beef of any silverskin and excess fat. Mix the olive oil, black pepper, and thyme. Rub the meat well all over with the mixture. Cover and marinate in the refrigerator for at least 2 hours, or up to 12 hours.

ARUGULA BUTTER

2 SHALLOTS, MINCED
½ CUP DRY WHITE WINE
2 TABLESPOONS WHITE WINE VINEGAR
1 CUP CHICKEN BROTH
½ CUP CHOPPED ARUGULA, PACKED
¼ CUP CHOPPED FRESH ITALIAN PARSLEY LEAVES, PACKED
2 TABLESPOONS CHOPPED FRESH CHIVES
2 TABLESPOONS CHOPPED FRESH BASIL LEAVES
3 TABLESPOONS UNSALTED BUTTER, SOFTENED
¼ CUP OLIVE OIL
SALT AND FRESH-GROUND PEPPER

Combine the shallots, white wine, and wine vinegar in a nonreactive saucepan. Reduce over medium heat to a scant tablespoon of liquid. Add the chicken broth and reduce by half. Cool the mixture to room temperature, then place it in a blender or food processor. Add the arugula, parsley, chives, basil, and butter. Turn on the motor, and drizzle in the olive oil to make an emulsion. Season with salt and pepper. Transfer the butter to a dish, cover, and refrigerate until ready to cook the beef.

CABERNET SAUVIGNON SAUCE

3 CUPS CABERNET SAUVIGNON

1 SHALLOT, MINCED

1 GARLIC CLOVE, MINCED

2 TABLESPOONS BALSAMIC VINEGAR

1 TABLESPOON FRESH THYME LEAVES

1 TOMATO, SEEDED AND DICED

3 CUPS BEEF BROTH

4 TABLESPOONS UNSALTED BUTTER

Remove the beef from the refrigerator 1 to 2 hours before you're ready to cook it and let it stand. Make the sauce base before cooking the meat. Combine the Cabernet Sauvignon, shallot, garlic, vinegar, thyme, and tomato in a nonreactive saucepan. Reduce by half over medium heat. Add the beef broth and reduce again by half. Strain the sauce base into a clean saucepan, reduce to about 1 cup and adjust the seasoning. Remove from the heat and reserve. Cut the butter into bits and reserve.

TO FINISH THE DISH

When ready to cook the filet, preheat the oven to 450° F. Remove the arugula butter from the refrigerator.

Salt the filet lightly and brown it well all over in a nonstick sauté pan. Place the filet on a rack in a roasting pan and roast until it is rare, about 20 to 25 minutes. Let the filet rest for at least 10 minutes before slicing.

While the meat is resting, finish the sauce with the butter. Heat the sauce base over low heat. Off the heat, swirl in the butter, two or three bits at a time. Keep the sauce in a warm place.

When ready to serve, divide the filet into six portions. Arrange the meat on serving plates or a platter. Surround with the Cabernet Sauvignon sauce and garnish each portion with a piece of the arugula butter.

PEAR HAZELNUT CUSTARD

Annie Roberts's fruit-and-nut combination desserts have the special quality of contrasting the sweet-tartness of the fruit with the milky sweetness of the nuts. This custard is particularly enjoyable with a dessert wine made with botrytised grapes, such as Sauvignon Blanc or Johannisberg Riesling, and is best served on the day it is made. You can make it in the morning, invert onto a serving platter, cool to room temperature, then refrigerate until about an hour before serving.

1 ½ POUNDS ANJOU OR WINTER BARTLETT OR NELIS PEARS

3 TABLESPOONS UNSALTED BUTTER

⅔ CUP SUGAR

¼ CUP DARK RUM

¾ CUP HAZELNUTS, LIGHTLY TOASTED (PAGE 120) AND SKINS RUBBED LOOSE

3 LARGE EGGS

1 CUP WHIPPING CREAM

PINCH SALT

¼ TEASPOON PURE VANILLA EXTRACT

Peel and core the pears. Slice them ¼ inch thick. Melt the butter in a sauté pan over medium heat. Add the sliced pears and cook for 2 minutes. Add ⅓ cup of the sugar and the rum. Cook the pears for about 3 minutes, stirring to coat with the sugar, until they are firm-tender. Remove from the heat and cool for 30 minutes.

Preheat the oven to 350° F. Lightly butter a 9-inch glass pie plate.

Grind the hazelnuts to a fine meal in a food processor with the remaining sugar. Drain the pears and add their liquid to the nuts. Add the eggs, cream, salt, and vanilla and stir to combine.

Arrange half of the pear slices concentrically on the bottom of the prepared pie plate. Pour the nut mixture over the pears. Cover the remaining pears with plastic wrap and reserve. Bake the custard in the center of the oven for 30 minutes, or until set.

Remove the custard from the oven and cool on a rack for 15 to 20 minutes. Loosen the edges with a knife or metal spatula and invert onto a serving platter. Arrange the remaining pear slices on top. Serve the custard slightly warm, or at room temperature, in wedges.

Winter Recipes

EGGNOG

Several members of the Mondavi family have taken on the holiday eggnog ritual, according to different formulas. Tim Mondavi describes the eggnog he has been making recently, and shares here a variation of Grandpa John's—his maternal grandfather's—recipe. "The way I've found to get the optimum flavor is to make the eggnog several days ahead; the ingredients have time to mellow and work together for a complex, smooth flavor. I like to whip in the egg whites and cream after the base is well chilled so that the cream doesn't rise. I stir the eggnog every day, taste, and add a little more brandy if it needs it." This eggnog could well convert even those who profess not to like eggnog; it is not cloying with a surfeit of sugar, eggs, or brandy. If you prefer a foamy eggnog, whip the cream and egg whites and stir them in several hours before serving. The recipe is easily doubled for larger gatherings. Because the egg yolks are cooked, the eggnog keeps well in the refrigerator.

5 LARGE EGGS, SEPARATED
½ CUP SUGAR
6 CUPS MILK
1 CUP BRANDY
1 TEASPOON PURE VANILLA EXTRACT
¼ CUP RUM
1 CUP WHIPPING CREAM
PINCH FRESH-GRATED NUTMEG

Place the egg yolks in a nonreactive saucepan and whisk them well with ¼ cup of the sugar. Whisk in the milk over low heat. Whisk in ½ cup of the brandy. Add the remaining sugar and the vanilla, stirring continually. When the sugar has dissolved, cool the mixture to room temperature, then refrigerate until well chilled.

Add the remaining brandy and the rum. Beat the egg whites until they are stiff, but not dry, and fold them into the eggnog. Beat the cream to soft peaks and fold it in. Add the nutmeg, stir well, and chill for at least several hours, preferably longer.

BUTTERNUT SQUASH SOUP WITH GINGER AND LIME

Annie Roberts combines these simple ingredients to create a thoroughly satisfying winter or autumn soup. The soup is light enough to precede almost any meal, but has enough body and flavor to enjoy with a glass of Fumé or Chenin Blanc.

1 MEDIUM-SIZE ONION, DICED FINE, ABOUT 1 CUP
1½ TABLESPOONS GRATED OR MINCED PEELED
   GINGERROOT
3 TABLESPOONS UNSALTED BUTTER
2 CUPS WATER

2 LARGE BUTTERNUT SQUASH, ABOUT 2 POUNDS,
   PEELED, SEEDED, AND SLICED THIN
2 CUPS CHICKEN BROTH
3 GARLIC CLOVES
ABOUT 2 TABLESPOONS LIME JUICE
SALT AND FRESH-GROUND PEPPER
1 LIME
⅓ CUP VEGETABLE OIL
ABOUT 1 OUNCE GINGERROOT, PEELED AND CUT IN
   FINE JULIENNE

In a nonreactive soup pot or large saucepan, cook the onion and grated gingerroot in the butter over low heat until the onion is soft, about 5 minutes. Add the water, squash, broth, and garlic.

Cover and bring the mixture to a boil. Reduce the heat to a simmer and cook until the squash is very tender, 15 to 20 minutes. Puree the mixture in batches in a blender or food processor.

Return the soup to the pan and season with about 2 tablespoons of lime juice, salt, and fresh-ground pepper. Reheat the soup gently while you prepare the garnish.

Cut 4 to 6 slices of lime as thin as you can. Heat the oil in a small skillet over medium-high heat until it is hot, but not smoking. Fry the julienned gingerroot in the oil until it is pale golden brown, about 30 seconds. Remove the gingerroot to paper towels to drain.

Serve the soup in warm soup plates or bowls. Float a slice of lime on each serving, and sprinkle with the fried gingerroot.

BLACK BEAN SOUP

SERVES 6 TO 8

If you want to make the soup in one day, Annie suggests you bring the beans to a boil in abundant water. Cook them for 5 minutes, then let them stand for an hour before draining and rinsing them. When she wants a thick soup, Annie purees half of the beans and vegetables.

1 POUND DRIED BLACK BEANS

¼ CUP OLIVE OIL

1 ONION, DICED

3 GARLIC CLOVES, CHOPPED

2 CARROTS, PEELED AND DICED

½ JALAPEÑO PEPPER, SEEDED AND DICED

1 TABLESPOON CUMIN SEEDS, LIGHTLY TOASTED IN A SMALL SKILLET AND GROUND

1 ½ TEASPOONS GROUND CARDAMOM

2 BAY LEAVES

1 ½ TEASPOONS CHILI POWDER, OR TO TASTE

1 CUP DRY WHITE WINE

4 CUPS CHICKEN BROTH

SALT AND FRESH-GROUND PEPPER

SPLASH OF WINE VINEGAR

GARNISH: SOUR CREAM AND DICED TOMATO

Wash and sort the beans. Soak the beans overnight in ample cold water, then drain and rinse.

Heat the oil in a soup pot over medium heat. Add the onion, garlic, carrots, and jalapeño. Lower the heat, cover the pot, and cook the vegetables until they are tender but not brown, 7 to 10 minutes. Add the cumin, cardamom, and bay leaves and cook for 2 minutes over medium heat. Stir in the chili powder and wine. Reduce the liquid by half.

Add the prepared beans and chicken broth. Bring the liquid to a boil, reduce the heat to a simmer, and skim off any foam. Cook the beans for about an hour, or until they are very tender. Season well with salt and pepper and add a splash of vinegar. Serve the soup hot, garnished with a little sour cream and diced tomato.

Margrit's Olive Rosemary Bread

Bread is one of the important basics of life for the Mondavis. In the last fifteen years or so, the Napa Valley, as well as other regions of the country, has been home to people who have dedicated themselves to the baker's art and craft, with the hard work and precision that the craft demands. Margrit often quadruples the recipe, setting aside a portion or two for this flavorful bread and baking the rest plain.

¼ CUP RYE FLOUR

1 CUP LUKEWARM (ABOUT 100° F) WATER

1 PACKAGE DRY YEAST

1 TEASPOON SALT

ABOUT 3 CUPS UNBLEACHED ALL-PURPOSE FLOUR

6 TO 8 KALAMATA OLIVES, PITTED AND CHOPPED

1 TABLESPOON CHOPPED FRESH ROSEMARY LEAVES

Mix the rye flour with the water in a mixing bowl. Stir in the yeast and let proof until the mixture becomes foamy, about 10 minutes. Stir in the salt.

Add 2 cups of flour and stir well. Add more flour, about ¼ cup at a time, stirring well after each addition until you have a smooth, soft dough. Turn the dough onto a lightly floured board and knead it for 4 minutes.

Lightly oil the bowl and place the dough in it. Cover the bowl with a damp cloth and let the dough rise in a warm place 2 hours, or until doubled in bulk.

Punch the dough down and let it rest 10 minutes. Preheat the oven to 450° F; lightly oil a 9 × 5-inch bread pan.

Flatten the dough to a rectangle, spread the olives and rosemary over it, and knead them into the dough. Shape the dough into a loaf and place it in the lightly oiled bread pan. Let rise in a warm place until almost doubled in bulk.

Bake the bread for 15 minutes, then reduce the heat to 375° F and bake for about 40 minutes longer, until it is golden brown and hollow-sounding when tapped. Turn the bread out of the pan onto a rack and cool for about 15 minutes before cutting. Or, cool to room temperature before cutting.

Leek, Prosciutto, and Red Pepper Croutons

Sweet, salt, and tangy flavors mingle in this appetizer that stimulates but does not satiate. Fumé Blanc and Chardonnay are wines that will complement the croutons. The leeks may be cooked a day ahead and brought to room temperature before assembling the croutons.

- 4 LEEKS, ABOUT 5 OUNCES EACH
- 2 TABLESPOONS EXTRA-VIRGIN OLIVE OIL
- 1 CUP DRY WHITE WINE, PREFERABLY CHARDONNAY
- 1 TABLESPOON CHOPPED FRESH MARJORAM LEAVES,
  OR 1½ TEASPOONS DRIED MARJORAM, CRUMBLED
- SALT AND FRESH-GROUND PEPPER
- 3 OUNCES PROSCIUTTO, SLICED THIN
- 1 BAGUETTE
- 1 SMALL RED BELL PEPPER, ABOUT 4 OUNCES,
  ROASTED (PAGE 133), PEELED, SEEDED, AND
  DICED
- OPTIONAL: 3 OUNCES FRESH MILD CHÈVRE
- 1 TABLESPOON CHOPPED ITALIAN PARSLEY LEAVES

Trim the leeks to the tender pale green and white. Halve the leeks lengthwise and rinse well between the layers to rid the leeks of any sand. Slice as thin as possible crosswise.

Heat the oil in a sauté pan over medium heat. Add the leeks and cook for about 5 minutes, stirring occasionally. Reduce the heat if necessary so the leeks do not brown.

Add the wine and marjoram, and season with salt and pepper. Reduce the heat and cook until the leeks are just tender, about 7 minutes.

Meanwhile, cut the prosciutto in a fine dice. Slice the baguette about ¼ inch thick and toast the slices.

When the leeks are done, stir in the prosciutto and let the mixture cool to room temperature. Add the red peppers, and crumble the chèvre into the mixture, if desired. Adjust the seasoning. Spread the mixture on the baguette slices and garnish with the chopped parsley. The croutons may be heated under the broiler for a minute or two, or served at room temperature.

Scallops with Truffles in Puff Pastry
Troigros

Pierre and Michel Troisgros recommend using the best preserved truffles you can find, or using fresh ones in season, usually available from France in December and January. When the Troisgros demonstrated this dish for the Great Chefs at the Robert Mondavi Winery Program, they chose a reserve Chardonnay to serve with it. The pastry may be rolled a day ahead, covered, and refrigerated. The court bouillon base for the sauce may be made a day ahead and refrigerated; it is best if it stands for at least 2 hours so the flavors come together.

Puff Pastry

12 OUNCES PUFF PASTRY DOUGH

Roll the pastry about 1/32 inch thick. If the pastry begins to pull back, let it rest in the refrigerator for 30 minutes before continuing. Cut into eighteen 4-inch rounds. Place the rounds on nonstick baking sheets, or ones lined with parchment paper. Cover with wax paper and refrigerate for at least an hour, or up to 4 hours.

Sauce

1 SMALL CARROT, ABOUT 2 OUNCES
6 RED PEARL ONIONS
1 GARLIC CLOVE
1 FRESH THYME SPRIG
1 BAY LEAF
1 TEASPOON MINCED GINGERROOT
¼ CUP DRY WHITE WINE
¼ CUP WATER
SALT AND FRESH-GROUND PEPPER
6 TABLESPOONS CHILLED UNSALTED BUTTER

Make the court bouillon base first. Slice the carrot thin. Peel the onions and slice them thin, then separate into rings. Slice the garlic thin.

Combine the vegetables in a saucepan, with the thyme, bay leaf, ginger, white wine, and water. Bring to a boil for 3 minutes, then remove from the heat and season with salt and pepper. Reserve. Cut the butter into bits and reserve, refrigerated.

Scallops and Assembly

2 OUNCES BLACK TRUFFLES
SALT AND FRESH-GROUND PEPPER
ABOUT TWENTY 2-INCH SPINACH LEAVES FROM
1 BUNCH SPINACH
18 ALASKAN SCALLOPS IN THE SHELL, ABOUT
1 OUNCE EACH , OR 4 OUNCES BAY SCALLOPS
1 EGG, LIGHTLY BEATEN
GARNISH: FRESH CHERVIL SPRIGS

Chop the truffles very fine and season them lightly with salt and pepper. Reserve them until ready to assemble the dish.

Trim and wash about 20 spinach leaves of about the same size, about 2 or 3 inches long. To blanch the spinach, place half of the leaves in a large strainer and blanch in boiling salted water for 2 seconds. Spread the leaves on kitchen or paper towels to dry. Repeat with the remaining spinach.

Remove the scallops from their shells and rinse under running water. Dry the scallops on kitchen or paper towels. Or, remove any tough tissue from the bay scallops, then rinse and dry them as above. Season the scallops lightly with salt and pepper.

To Assemble the Dish

When ready to assemble the dish, preheat the oven to 450° F. Discard the herbs from the court bouillon. Have ready six warm serving plates. Brush the edges of the puff pastry with the egg wash.

Roll the scallops in the truffle, then wrap them in spinach leaves, one scallop for each spinach leaf. Place each bundle in the center of a puff paste round and bring the edges up and around to form a little purse shape. Pinch the pastry closed in the center. Place each pastry, after it is shaped, on a baking sheet. When all the pastries are formed, brush them lightly with the egg wash on the sides and top. Bake the pastries for 7 to 10 minutes, until they are golden brown.

While the pastries are baking, finish the sauce. Reheat the court bouillon base over high heat. Incorporate the butter by swirling, not whisking, in one or two small pieces at a time.

To serve, divide the sauce among the warm serving plates. Place the scallop purses on top and garnish with chervil sprigs. Serve immediately.

CHICKEN BREASTS WITH CHARDONNAY AND TARRAGON

SERVES 4

Though the preparation is simple, the flavors are pronounced in this chicken dish for Chardonnay lovers created by Sarah Scott, executive chef at the Food and Wine Center at Costa Mesa. Sautéed Spinach with Garlic (page 71), or other winter greens, and couscous make good side dishes.

- 2 WHOLE BONED CHICKEN BREASTS, WITH SKIN
- 4 OUNCES EMMENTAL OR GRUYÈRE CHEESE, GRATED
- SALT AND FRESH-GROUND PEPPER
- 1 CUP CHARDONNAY
- 3 SHALLOTS, DICED FINE
- 1 CUP WHIPPING CREAM
- ½ CUP CHICKEN BROTH
- 1 TEASPOON DRIED TARRAGON
- ½ TEASPOON MUSTARD SEED
- ½ TEASPOON MUSTARD POWDER
- ½ TEASPOON GRATED LEMON ZEST
- ½ TEASPOON CRACKED BLACK PEPPER

Loosen the skins of the chicken breasts. Place the grated cheese evenly under the skins and pat down. Place the chicken in a buttered or parchment-lined shallow baking pan. Salt and pepper the chicken lightly on both sides and reserve.

Preheat the oven to 375° F.

Combine the Chardonnay, shallots, cream, and chicken broth in a nonreactive saucepan. Cook over medium-high heat until the mixture begins to thicken, about 5 minutes. Whisk in the tarragon, mustard seed and powder, lemon zest, and cracked pepper. Reduce over medium-high heat until the sauce is the consistency of light cream, about 15 minutes. Adjust the seasoning with salt and pepper.

Pour the sauce over the chicken and bake until the chicken is just cooked through, about 25 minutes. Serve hot.

Lamb Shanks with Red Wine and White Beans

SERVES 8

Annie Roberts likes to use cannellini beans in this dish, since they keep their shape and have a lovely creamy texture. Use navy or other white beans if you like. Cooking times of beans vary; watch so that beans are not overcooked. The dish may be prepared a day or two ahead, brought to room temperature, and gently reheated. Gremolata, the classic Italian lemon, parsley, and garlic mixture for garnishing veal stews, works very well with lamb, too.

- **12** OUNCES DRIED WHITE BEANS, SOAKED OVERNIGHT
- **8** GARLIC CLOVES
- **4** TABLESPOONS OLIVE OIL
- **2** MEDIUM-SIZE ONIONS, HALVED AND SLICED THIN
- SALT AND FRESH-GROUND PEPPER
- **8** LAMB SHANKS FROM THE FORESHANK, EACH CUT INTO 2 PIECES
- **2** CUPS DRY RED WINE
- **4** CUPS CHICKEN BROTH
- ABOUT 4 CUPS LAMB STOCK (RECIPE FOLLOWS)
- **4** FRESH THYME SPRIGS
- **1** BAY LEAF
- **20** FRESH ITALIAN PARSLEY SPRIGS
- **1** POUND FRESH TOMATOES, CORED, SEEDED, AND CHOPPED, OR ONE 14-OUNCE CAN DICED TOMATOES
- **3** LEMONS

Rinse the beans and place them in a pot. Just cover with cold water and bring to a boil over medium heat. Reduce the heat to low, cover the pot, and simmer until just firm-tender, about 30 to 45 minutes.

Meanwhile, slice 4 of the garlic cloves thin. Heat 2 tablespoons of the olive oil in a large sauté pan or casserole over medium heat. Add the onions and the sliced garlic and cook about 8 minutes, until the vegetables are golden. Remove to a plate and reserve.

Salt and pepper the lamb shanks lightly. Add the remaining olive oil to the pan and brown the lamb shanks, in two batches if necessary, on all sides over high heat. Remove the shanks from the pan and add the wine. Heat the wine, scraping up the browned bits from the bottom of the pan.

Return the shanks, onions, and garlic to the pan. Add the chicken broth, 2 cups of the lamb stock, the thyme, bay leaf, and 4 parsley sprigs. Cover and simmer for 1½ hours, or until the lamb is tender.

Remove the lamb and let the broth stand at room temperature for 20 to 30 minutes. Skim the fat from the broth and season well with salt and pepper. Return the lamb to the pot along with the beans and tomatoes and simmer for 20 minutes, uncovered. Adjust the seasoning, and add a little lamb stock if necessary.

Meanwhile, remove the zest from the lemons and the leaves from the remaining parsley sprigs. Slice the remaining garlic thin. Mince the lemon zest, parsley, and garlic together.

To serve, place two pieces of lamb shank for each serving in a soup plate; add beans and broth. Garnish with the lemon, parsley, and garlic mixture.

LAMB STOCK

4 TO 5 POUNDS LAMB BONES AND TRIMMINGS, OR
    LAMB STEW MEAT WITH BONES

2 CUPS DRY WHITE OR RED WINE

1 ONION, QUARTERED

2 SHALLOTS, SLICED THICK

1 CELERY STALK, CHOPPED COARSE

1 CARROT, CHOPPED COARSE

4 OUNCES MUSHROOMS, SLICED THICK

BOUQUET GARNI: 5 OR 6 FRESH ITALIAN PARSLEY
    SPRIGS, 3 OR 4 FRESH THYME SPRIGS, 1 BAY LEAF

OPTIONAL: 1 RIPE TOMATO, QUARTERED

Preheat the oven to 450° F.

Place the lamb in a roasting pan in one layer and roast until the lamb is well browned, about 30 minutes, turning once. Deglaze the roasting pan with the wine and place the bones and pan juices in a stockpot.

Add the vegetables, bouquet garni, and tomato, if desired. Barely cover the meat and vegetables with cold water. Bring the stock to a boil and skim it immediately. Reduce to a strong simmer, skimming the surface frequently for 2 hours, and occasionally for another 2 hours.

Strain the stock and cool to room temperature. Refrigerate the stock and remove any fat. The stock can be reduced to a demiglace, which can be frozen for several months.

ANNIE ROBERTS'S RISOTTO

Annie's excellent risotto can be served Italian style, in small portions as a first course, or as a side dish with simple roasts and grills. If you serve it as a first course, the wine to accompany should be the one you use in the risotto.

6 CUPS CHICKEN BROTH

4 TABLESPOONS UNSALTED BUTTER

1 SMALL ONION, DICED

2 CUPS ARBORIO RICE

1 CUP DRY WHITE WINE

¼ CUP CHOPPED FRESH CHIVES

½ CUP FRESH-GRATED PARMESAN CHEESE

SALT AND FRESH-GROUND PEPPER

Heat the chicken broth and keep it warm while starting the risotto.

Melt the butter over medium heat in a large saucepan or casserole. Add the onion and cook for 3 minutes; do not brown. Stir in the rice and cook for about 5 minutes, stirring continuously to warm each grain. Add the wine and cook until it has been absorbed by the rice. Add enough broth to just cover the rice.

Adjust the heat so that bubbles just break the surface. Add about a cup of broth as the previous broth is absorbed. Stir frequently, adding broth as necessary, until the rice is tender but firm, 15 to 18 minutes.

Stir in the chives and cheese and season to taste with salt and pepper. Serve hot.

ROAST VEAL LOIN WITH CHARD OR MUSHROOMS

Chef Gary Jenanyan likes to use red or green chard or mushrooms as a stuffing for this impressive main course. The recipe gives instructions for using chard; if you would like to try mushrooms, you will need 12 ounces of them and ½ cup chopped Italian parsley. After trimming the mushrooms, mince them in a food processor. Add the mushrooms to the shallots, garlic, and rosemary and proceed with the recipe. Add the parsley when you combine all the stuffing ingredients.

A good butcher makes the preparation of the veal relatively simple. Ask your butcher to bone a veal short loin of about 6 pounds, and trim it of fat and connective tissue. Have him keep the tenderloin separate and butterfly the loin to give you a piece of veal about 10 by 14 inches and ½ inch thick, weighing between 3 and 3¼ pounds. Have him grind the lean trim from the flank section and other pieces, which should weigh about 8 ounces.

1 VEAL SHORT LOIN, WITH TENDERLOIN AND GROUND LEAN TRIMMINGS RESERVED

SALT AND FRESH-GROUND PEPPER

1 POUND RED OR GREEN CHARD, LEAVES AND STEMS SEPARATED

6 TABLESPOONS UNSALTED BUTTER

3 SHALLOTS, MINCED

3 FRESH ROSEMARY SPRIGS, ABOUT 3 INCHES EACH, LEAVES MINCED

2 GARLIC CLOVES, MINCED

1 LARGE EGG

½ CUP MILK

½ CUP FINE DRY BREAD CRUMBS

2 TABLESPOONS CANOLA, OR OTHER VEGETABLE OIL

1 MEDIUM-SIZE CARROT, DICED

2 MEDIUM-SIZE ONIONS, DICED

1 CUP CHARDONNAY

2 CUPS CHICKEN BROTH

Season the veal with salt and pepper. Cut the tenderloin in half lengthwise. Reserve the meat at room temperature while you prepare the stuffing.

Blanch the chard leaves until just tender, about 4 minutes. Reserve the stems for another use. Refresh the leaves with cold water, dry well, and chop fine.

Melt 4 tablespoons of the butter in a sauté pan and add the shallots. Cook over low heat until they have softened, about 5 minutes. Add the garlic and rosemary to the shallots and cook another minute. Add the chard and cook until the juices have evaporated, about 5 minutes, stirring well. Season with salt and pepper.

Place the ground veal in a large mixing bowl. Add the chard mixture and blend thoroughly. Add the egg, milk, and bread crumbs and combine thoroughly. The stuffing should be moist and able to hold together. Season the mixture very well.

Preheat the oven to 400° F. Spread the stuffing mixture evenly over half the length of the veal loin. Place the tenderloin pieces in the center of the stuffing, overlapping the thin ends. Roll the loin and stuffing over itself like a jelly roll with the tenderloin in the center. Tie the roast at 2-inch intervals.

Heat the remaining butter with the oil in a roasting pan that has a rack. Add the roast to the fat and brown on all sides over high heat. Remove the roast to the rack. Drain the fat from the pan and add the carrot, onions, Chardonnay, and chicken broth to the pan. Place the veal roast, on the rack, in the pan.

Cook the roast for 40 minutes, or until the internal temperature is 130° to 135° F. Remove the roast from the oven and let rest for at least 10 minutes. Meanwhile, strain the pan juices into a saucepan, pressing on the vegetables. Adjust the seasoning and heat while you slice the roast.

To serve, untie the roast and cut into approximately ½-inch slices. Place on warm plates or platter and moisten with the sauce. Serve immediately, and pass the remaining sauce.

CELERY ROOT AND POTATO PUREE

SERVES 6

As Margrit says of this recipe, "It's delicious!" Since it looks very much like mashed potatoes, most people are pleasantly surprised by the slightly tangy flavor. The puree accompanies many main courses well, particularly roasts with pan juices or reduction sauces, such as Rack of Lamb with Herb Crust (page 161) and Roast Veal Loin with Chard or Mushrooms (opposite). The dish may be made several hours ahead and gently reheated.

1 ¼ POUNDS RUSSET POTATOES

2 POUNDS CELERY ROOT

SALT

½ CUP WHIPPING CREAM

3 TABLESPOONS UNSALTED BUTTER, CUT IN BITS

1 TO 2 TABLESPOONS LEMON JUICE

FRESH-GROUND PEPPER

Peel the potatoes and cut them into about 1-inch pieces. Place them in a nonreactive pan and just cover with cold water. Trim the celery root of the tough outer layer of skin and cut into about 1-inch pieces. Add the celery root to the potatoes and barely cover with water.

Add about a teaspoon of salt to the potatoes and celery root and cook the vegetables until they are soft, about 15 minutes.

Drain the vegetables and place them back in the pot. Stir in the cream and simmer gently for about 10 minutes, stirring frequently to prevent sticking. Stir in the butter and remove from the heat.

Put the mixture through a potato ricer, or pulse in a food processor until almost smooth, retaining some bits of celery root and potato. Or, mash the mixture with a potato masher to a rough puree, then whisk briefly with a whisk or hand-held electric mixer to make fluffy.

Stir in the lemon juice and adjust the seasoning with salt and pepper. Serve hot.

ALMOND ICE CREAM

To provide a contrast to the nuttiness of this ice cream—an Annie Roberts recipe—pair it with the tangy flavor of blood oranges. A simple syrup of blood orange juice and a little sugar makes a pretty and tasty presentation. Or, serve the ice cream with a not-too-sweet cookie, such as the Kolakis (page 98).

2 CUPS SLICED ALMONDS
1 CUP SUGAR
2 CUPS WHIPPING CREAM
1 CUP MILK
3 LARGE EGG YOLKS

Spread the almonds on a baking sheet and toast them to medium-golden brown in a 350° F oven, about 7 minutes. Let the almonds cool to room temperature.

Combine the almonds and sugar in a food processor. Process to a medium-fine meal.

In a heavy-bottomed saucepan, combine the whipping cream and milk. Add the nut-sugar mixture and stir well. Heat the mixture to just scalding over medium-low heat. Remove from the heat and let steep for 30 minutes.

Strain the mixture through a fine strainer into a bowl. Whisk the egg yolks lightly in a separate bowl, and gradually whisk in the almond cream. Return the mixture to the saucepan and cook over medium-low heat until the mixture just coats the back of a metal spoon, about 5 minutes, stirring constantly.

Strain the mixture into a bowl set in a larger bowl half filled with ice water. Chill thoroughly, stirring frequently. Freeze in an ice cream maker following manufacturer's instructions. Or, refrigerate up to 24 hours, until you are ready to freeze the ice cream.

GRANDMA'S POUND CAKE
WITH WINTER FRUIT SALAD

Margrit has been making this cake from her grandmother's recipe for many years and likes to serve it with fruit salad made with whatever fresh fruit is available. "I choose the best winter fruit," she says, "such as apples, bananas, oranges, pears, or tangerines, peel and cut them in small pieces, then toss them with the juice of a Meyer lemon, and a teaspoon of sugar if necessary."

To help the eggs aerate, and the cake to be light, warm the eggs in hot tap water. For this recipe you will need a 2-quart Bundt pan or a loaf pan exactly 9 × 5 inches. A glass or ceramic pan results in longer cooking time and a more deeply browned crust.

1 CUP (8 OUNCES) UNSALTED BUTTER, SOFTENED
1½ CUPS SUGAR
6 LARGE EGGS, AT WARM ROOM TEMPERATURE
1 TEASPOON PURE VANILLA EXTRACT
ZEST OF 1 LEMON, MINCED
2 TABLESPOONS COGNAC OR BRANDY
½ TEASPOON SALT
2 CUPS SIFTED UNBLEACHED ALL-PURPOSE FLOUR
OPTIONAL: FRUIT SALAD MADE WITH WINTER FRUITS
   OF CHOICE

Preheat the oven to 325° F. Butter and lightly flour a 2-quart Bundt pan or a 9 × 5-inch loaf pan.

Beat the butter very well, about 5 minutes, in a large bowl with an electric mixer. Add the sugar and beat very well, 5 to 8 minutes, until very light and fluffy. Add the eggs, one a time, beating well after each addition, and scraping the sides and bottom of the bowl. Add the vanilla, lemon zest, Cognac, and salt and beat well.

Fold the flour into the mixture in four additions. Pour the batter into the prepared pan and bake for 1 hour to 1 hour and 20 minutes, or until a cake tester or toothpick inserted in the center comes out clean.

Cool the cake in the pan on a rack for 20 minutes. Turn the cake out and serve warm or at room temperature, accompanied by fruit salad, if desired.

CHOCOLATE CASSIS TRUFFLES
MAKES ABOUT 50 TRUFFLES

The touch of cassis gives the truffles a berry flavor that goes well with Cabernet Sauvignon. Michael Chipchase doubles the recipe when he is serving large parties in the Vineyard Room at the winery. The truffles keep well, refrigerated in single layers, for 2 or 3 days.

- ½ CUP HEAVY CREAM
- 4 OUNCES BITTERSWEET CHOCOLATE, CHOPPED COARSE
- 4 OUNCES SEMISWEET CHOCOLATE, CHOPPED COARSE
- 4 TABLESPOONS UNSALTED BUTTER, CUT INTO BITS
- ¼ CUP CRÈME DE CASSIS
- 1 CUP UNSWEETENED COCOA POWDER, SIFTED
- ABOUT 50 SMALL PAPER CANDY CUPS

Place the cream in a heavy saucepan and heat it thoroughly over medium-low heat, but do not allow it to boil. When it is hot, reduce the heat to low and add both chocolates, whisking continually to incorporate. Whisk in the butter. When the mixture is completely smooth, remove it from the heat and whisk in the crème de cassis.

Pour the mixture into a glass dish and cool to room temperature. Cover with plastic wrap and refrigerate for at least 4 hours, or until the mixture is very firm.

Using a small melon baller or spoon, scoop small pieces of the truffle mixture and roll quickly between your palms to form round truffles. Roll the truffles as

they are formed in the cocoa powder. Shake off excess cocoa powder, and place the truffles in the candy cups. Refrigerate until ready to serve.

FOR VINTNERS, SPRING IS THE

SPRING

SEASON OF MAXIMUM ACTIVITY

MUSTARD AND POPPIES LIVEN THE FIELDS, FORSYTHIA

and flowering plum branches scent the corner

flower shop: Flowers and plants inform us of

spring's arrival even before we know it in our

bones. They respond to the subtle spinning of

the earth and the slight increases of moisture

and warmth that can happen well before calen-

dar spring. But being so quick to respond has its dangers. In Napa Valley the weather is usually more settled than many places where wine grapes are grown, but through May a watch is kept for frosts that can decimate the crop of buds that flower into grapes.

For vintners, spring is the season of maximum activity and vigilance in tending the vines. Budbreak usually comes in March, and buds are susceptible to a serious disease problem in the valley, powdery mildew. Wettable sulfur, which inhibits the growth of mildew but does not kill it, must be applied. Disking or mowing between the rows must be done to keep the mustard, grasses, and other plants from competing with the vines. New leaf growth is analyzed for deficiencies, and minerals or elements are applied if necessary.

At the Forni-Brown Gardens in Calistoga, Peter Forni, Lynn Brown, and Barney Welsh are also watching weather. After a brief close from about New Year's Day to Valentine's Day, these produce growers offer their flavorful, organically grown lettuces, salad greens, and herbs to an eager public that includes many of the valley's fine restaurants and wineries. Forni-Brown works closely with chefs to provide a wide variety of seasonal vegetables, including Oriental greens and herbs, heirloom tomatoes, a dozen or so lettuces, and several kinds of radicchio.

The Vineyard Room kitchen depends on its own garden as well as outside producers for tender chives, tarragon, sorrel and parsley, borage, nasturtium, and viola flowers for garnishes. The chefs can once again create dishes with artichokes, asparagus, early green beans, and watercress from the several nearby valleys

that border the ocean. It is still cool enough to

enjoy complex red wines with hearty main

courses, yet end with strawberries or rhubarb

and a light dessert wine to preview the next

season.

Wine and Food Pairing at Costa Mesa

Fire-Roasted Eggplant and Pepper Soup

FUMÉ BLANC

Pine Nut and
Basil-Crusted Salmon
with Chardonnay Sauce

CHARDONNAY

Mashed Potatoes with Caramelized Onions

Grilled Leg of Lamb with
Pinot Noir Sauce

PINOT NOIR OR CABERNET SAUVIGNON

Roasted Beets, Carrots in Broth,
and Pan-Steamed Asparagus

Rhubarb Meringue Tartlets with Strawberries

MOSCATO D'ORO OR SAUVIGNON BLANC BOTRYTIS

ood and wine pairings are, in the end, dependent on individual palates. Beyond the nuances and subtleties, as Margrit puts it, are the basic human elements that encompass food and wine. "We can learn to appreciate good simple food—good bread, food from the garden—and bring out a good bottle, a well-made wine. We can make a feast, no matter how simple the food and wine. When anyone takes the care to cook something good or make a good wine and share it with family and friends around the table, peoples' lives are enriched with happy moments."

hef Sarah Scott developed a wide-ranging menu to illustrate the possibilities of food and wine pairing and the transitional character of the seasons in southern California. The dishes were composed of ingredients available in late winter in the warm coastal regions of the country, and in early or mid-spring in other areas. Each dish can be combined with others you like for the season in your climate.

argrit and Sarah pointed out some helpful insights into selecting wines for dishes with collegial ease and joint expertise. Commonsensically, lighter wines—sparkling and still white varietals such as Fumé Blanc and Johannisberg Riesling—are best served first. They help wake the appetite and don't saturate the palate. The first course or appetizer, whether served with wine or not, starts the gastric juices flowing, so it's important to serve the next course within twenty minutes. There are two basic ways to work with wine and food—to match flavor characteristics or counterpoint them. Typically, wines will have flavors that largely match, but provide some counterpoint, or vice versa. In the case of the roasted vegetable soup, Fumé Blanc matches the ingredients with its vegetal character, but has a more lemony quality and a bit of spiciness. The palate picks up these contrasts as interesting and pleasant.

The buttery quality of the salmon and pine nuts finds a match in Chardonnay; Fumé Blanc is usually overcome by salmon, unless it is an especially deep reserve-quality wine. Chardonnay also has some bright fruit-acid, characterized most often as pineapplelike. The palate perceives this as providing contrast to the rich fish flavor. Sarah developed this recipe for the Mondavi Coastal Chardonnay, which is well-balanced between buttery and fruit-acid aspects.

For many people, the perfect wine to serve with lamb is Pinot Noir, for its hint of gaminess matches that of lamb. Pinot also has elements of fruit such as cherry, and many like that accented fruitiness with lamb. But other palates, including Margrit's focus on lamb's depth of flavor, which finds a complement in Cabernet Sauvignon. They find the contrast of Cabernet's tannins with lamb's tendency to coat the palate pleasing. Lamb pairs beautifully with many herbs, and Cabernet has some herbaceous tones that echo this, particularly when the dish has mint, rosemary, or basil.

For the Rhubarb Meringue Tartlets with Strawberries, Sarah chose a Moscato d'Oro to highlight the fruit. The meringue itself is rather neutral and light, which also works well with this wine. Moscato d'Oro is not aged in wood, and has a very refreshing fresh fruit character. She could also have chosen a denser botrytised wine, such as Sauvignon Blanc or Johannisberg Riesling to accent the curd, which is made with sugar, butter, and eggs, as well as rhubarb.

FIRE-ROASTED EGGPLANT AND PEPPER SOUP   SERVES 8

As Sarah explained, "When all the flavor elements—sweet, sour, salt, and bitter—are together in balance is when people say 'That's good.'" She created this soup with the sweetness of the onions, sourness of vinegar and lemon juice, salt, and slight bitterness of fire-roasted vegetables. Sometimes a small pinch of sugar is needed to bring the sweet element into balance. The strong vegetable components of the soup make Fumé Blanc, which has a somewhat vegetal character, a good wine complement. The garlic-spice oil can be used as a flavor-enhancing condiment in other soups, sauces, marinades, and vinaigrettes. Make it ahead and store it in the refrigerator for up to 5 days. You can also make the soup ahead and reheat it to serve.

GARLIC-SPICE OIL

   1 TEASPOON FENNEL SEEDS
 ½ TEASPOON CORIANDER SEEDS
 ½ TEASPOON CUMIN SEEDS
   2 HEADS GARLIC, PEELED
   1 CUP OLIVE OIL

Crush the fennel, coriander, and cumin seeds lightly with a heavy pot. Place the seeds in a small heavy-bottomed sauté pan and place over medium-low heat. Cook until the spices give off aroma, 3 to 5 minutes, shaking the pan frequently. Do not allow the spices to become overtoasted or they will be acrid.

Add the peeled garlic and stir in the olive oil. Turn the heat very low and cook for 20 to 30 minutes, or until the garlic cloves begin to shrivel and turn slightly brown. Watch carefully; the garlic can burn quickly once it begins to brown.

Remove the oil from the heat and let steep until the oil reaches room temperature. Strain the oil and reserve. Pick the soft garlic cloves from the strainer and mash or puree to a smooth paste. Reserve the garlic paste.

Soup

2 EGGPLANTS, ENDS TRIMMED

2 RED ONIONS WITH SKINS ON, HALVED CROSSWISE

2 YELLOW ONIONS WITH SKINS ON, HALVED CROSSWISE

3 RIPE TOMATOES, HALVED CROSSWISE AND SQUEEZED TO REMOVE SEEDS AND JUICE

2 RED BELL PEPPERS

2 YELLOW BELL PEPPERS

RESERVED GARLIC PASTE FROM GARLIC-SPICE OIL

8 CUPS CHICKEN BROTH

SPLASH OF SHERRY OR BALSAMIC VINEGAR

1 LEMON

SALT AND FRESH-GROUND PEPPER

Preheat the oven to 350° F.

Char the eggplants lightly over a gas flame for extra depth of flavor. Halve the eggplants lengthwise. Brush the cut surfaces with the garlic-spice oil and place, cut side down, on a parchment-lined baking sheet. Brush the cut surfaces of the onions and tomatoes with the oil and place them, cut side down, on the baking sheet.

Bake the vegetables for 45 to 50 minutes, or until the eggplant is soft, the flesh of the onions has pushed through the skins and is soft and caramelized, and the tomatoes are blackened and collapsed. Set the vegetables aside to cool.

Meanwhile, roast the peppers over a gas flame until they are well blackened all over. Place them in a paper bag to steam-loosen the skins. When the peppers are cool enough to handle, remove most of the blackened skin, leaving a few bits for flavor, and remove the stems, seeds, and veins.

When the baked vegetables are cool enough to handle, scoop the eggplant flesh from the skin and place in a blender or food processor. Remove the skins from the onions, and add the flesh to the eggplants. Remove the tomato skins and add the flesh and any pan juices to the eggplants and onions.

Add the garlic paste, roasted peppers, and 2 cups of chicken broth to the vegetables. Puree until smooth, adding more broth if necessary. The mixture should have the consistency of a slightly thickened cream soup.

Taste the soup and begin to season, adding a tablespoon or so of the garlic-spice oil, a small splash of vinegar, the juice of half the lemon, and salt and pepper. Work with all the seasonings until you have the flavor balance you like.

Heat the soup and adjust the seasonings, if necessary. Serve hot.

PINE NUT AND BASIL-CRUSTED SALMON WITH CHARDONNAY SAUCE

Sarah served this lovely salmon dish and its companion recipe of Mashed Potatoes with Caramelized Onions in small portions at the Wine Pairing so that guests could taste the way in which the fish, nuts, basil, and sauce complement the buttery quality of Chardonnay. The recipe serves 8 as a main course.

1 SIDE OF SALMON FILLET, ABOUT 3 POUNDS, SKINNED AND BONED

SALT AND FRESH-GROUND PEPPER

ABOUT ⅓ CUP OLIVE OIL

1 CUP PINE NUTS

1½ CUPS FRESH BASIL LEAVES

2 TABLESPOONS ALL-PURPOSE FLOUR

2 SHALLOTS, MINCED

1½ CUPS CHARDONNAY

¼ CUP HEAVY CREAM

6 TABLESPOONS UNSALTED BUTTER, CUT IN BITS

ABOUT 1 TABLESPOON LEMON JUICE

OPTIONAL: MASHED POTATOES AND CARAMELIZED ONIONS (RECIPE FOLLOWS)

Portion the salmon into eight 6-ounce pieces, or have your fishmonger do this; season lightly with salt and pepper and brush the top sides lightly with some of the olive oil.

Chop the pine nuts very fine with a sharp knife, or carefully in the food processor. Mince 1 cup of the basil leaves and mix with the pine nuts and flour in a wide bowl. Pat the pine nut–basil mixture onto the oiled salmon, covering the fish evenly. Cover loosely with plastic wrap and set aside while you make the sauce.

Combine the shallots, Chardonnay, and cream in a nonreactive saucepan. Reduce over high heat to about ¼ cup liquid. Reduce the heat to medium-low and whisk in the butter, a few bits at a time, until the butter is used up and the sauce has emulsified. Season with salt, pepper, and lemon juice. Remove from the heat and keep in a warm place until ready to serve the salmon.

When ready to serve, preheat the oven to 400° F. Line a baking sheet with parchment paper.

Heat the remaining oil in a 12-inch nonstick skillet over medium heat, or divide it among two smaller nonstick skillets if you don't have such a large one. Gently place the salmon, crust side down, in the pan. Cook until the crusts are golden brown, about 5 minutes, changing the position of the fillets carefully with a spatula for even browning.

Seasons of the Vineyard

134

Transfer the fillets, crust side up, to the prepared baking sheet. Bake until the salmon is just cooked through but still slightly translucent in the center, about 5 minutes.

Serve the salmon hot, on a bed of the hot mashed potatoes, or with another accompaniment. Reheat the sauce if necessary over low heat while the salmon is baking, and surround the salmon with the sauce. Garnish with the remaining ½ cup basil leaves, shredded fine.

MASHED POTATOES WITH CARAMELIZED ONIONS
SERVES 8

Here sweet onions such as Walla Walla, Maui, Vidalia, or Texas Sweet are best for a flavor that contrasts with the potatoes and Chardonnay.

6 RUSSET POTATOES, ABOUT 2½ POUNDS
8 TO 10 TABLESPOONS UNSALTED BUTTER
ABOUT ½ CUP MILK
SALT AND FRESH-GROUND PEPPER
2 SWEET ONIONS, ABOUT 8 OUNCES EACH
¼ CUP CHARDONNAY

Peel and quarter the potatoes. Boil them in lightly salted water until they are tender. Drain and return them to the pan. Mash the potatoes with 4 tablespoons of the butter, and add milk to the consistency you like. Season with salt and pepper and keep warm.

While the potatoes are boiling, halve the onions lengthwise and slice them thin crosswise. Melt 4 tablespoons butter in a sauté pan over medium heat. Add the onions and stir them occasionally until they begin to caramelize, about 10 minutes. Lower the heat, add the wine, and cook the onions until they are golden brown, about 20 minutes, stirring frequently. Stir the onions into the potatoes, adjust the seasoning, and add more butter, if you like. Serve hot.

Grilled Leg of Lamb with Pinot Noir Sauce

Sarah cuts the lamb into its natural muscle separations, which allows all pieces to be grilled to the same doneness. You can ask your butcher to follow this technique, called seaming, as well as to saw the bones into about 4-inch pieces for the stock. For best flavor and ease of preparation, marinate the lamb and make the stock a day ahead. A recipe for lamb stock is on page 117. Sarah suggests using an instant-read meat thermometer to check the doneness of the lamb; a reading of 125° F means the lamb is medium-rare. She likes to serve the lamb with the early spring vegetables in the following recipe.

Lamb

- **1 LEG OF LAMB, ABOUT 6 POUNDS, BONED**
- **1 HEAD GARLIC, PEELED AND SLIVERED**

½ CUP CHOPPED FRESH MIXED HERBS (ROSEMARY, THYME, CHIVES, PARSLEY, AND BASIL)

1 TABLESPOON CRUSHED FENNEL SEEDS

¼ CUP EXTRA-VIRGIN OLIVE OIL

FRESH-GROUND PEPPER

Cut the lamb into its natural muscle pieces. Combine the garlic, herbs, fennel seeds, and olive oil in a small bowl. Add a few grinds of pepper, then rub the marinade all over the meat. Cover and refrigerate at least 2 hours, or preferably overnight.

PINOT NOIR SAUCE

2 SHALLOTS, MINCED

2 GARLIC CLOVES, MINCED

1 TABLESPOON OLIVE OIL

4 OUNCES MUSHROOMS, CLEANED AND SLICED

½ BOTTLE (375 ML) PINOT NOIR

4 CUPS LAMB STOCK, (PAGE 117)

SALT AND FRESH-GROUND PEPPER

ROASTED BEETS, CARROTS IN BROTH, AND PAN-STEAMED ASPARAGUS (RECIPE FOLLOWS)

Soften the shallots and garlic in the olive oil in a sauté pan over medium heat. Add the mushrooms and increase the heat. Cook the mushrooms about 5 minutes, until their liquid has evaporated. Deglaze with the Pinot Noir, bring to a boil, lower the heat to a strong simmer, and reduce the liquid by half.

Add the lamb stock and again reduce by half. Strain the sauce into a clean pan, pressing on the vegetables, and taste for seasoning. The sauce may be reduced further if necessary. Add salt and pepper when you have finished the reduction.

TO FINISH THE LAMB

Remove the lamb from the refrigerator at least 2 hours before serving. Prepare the Roasted Beets, Carrots in Broth, and Pan-Steamed Asparagus (recipe follows) in the meantime.

When near serving time, prepare a grill, preferably with mesquite charcoal. When the coals are medium hot, place the lamb on the grill and cook, turning occasionally, until the lamb is rare to medium-rare. The smaller cuts will be done in about 8 minutes, the larger ones in about 20 minutes.

Allow the lamb to stand at room temperature about 10 minutes before carving. Meanwhile, heat the sauce. When ready to serve, carve the lamb in thin slices on a diagonal and place on a warm platter or plates. Arrange the vegetables around the lamb and spoon some hot sauce over both. Serve immediately, and pass the remaining sauce.

ROASTED BEETS, CARROTS IN BROTH, AND PAN-STEAMED ASPARAGUS

SERVES 6 TO 8

The beets may be roasted early in the day and held at cool room temperature. They may be wrapped in foil and reheated in the oven before serving. The carrots may be braised early in the day, undercooking them a little, and just heated through before serving. The asparagus is best cooked not more than an hour before serving.

1   BUNCH BEETS, ABOUT 2 INCHES IN DIAMETER
1   BUNCH CARROTS WITH TOPS
1   CUP CHICKEN BROTH
1 ½   POUNDS ASPARAGUS, PENCIL-THIN IF POSSIBLE
2   TABLESPOONS UNSALTED BUTTER

Preheat the oven to 400° F. Trim the beets, leaving about an inch of stems and tails. Scrub the beets well and wrap each beet tightly in doubled aluminum foil. Place the beets in a baking dish and roast for about an hour, until tender when gently squeezed with a pot holder.

Remove the beets from the dish and let stand until cool enough to handle. Remove the foil and trim and peel the beets; the skins will slip off when rubbed with the fingers. Cut the beets into rounds, half rounds, or dice, then place in a baking dish, cover tightly with foil, and reserve until ready to serve.

Peel the carrots and trim the tops to about 1½ inches. If the carrots are unevenly sized, or thicker than about ½ inch, cut and trim them so they will cook in the same amount of time.

Add the carrots to a saute pan with the chicken broth. Cover the pan and bring the liquid to a boil. Immediately reduce the heat to a simmer and cook the carrots until just crisp-tender, about 5 minutes. Remove from the heat, and remove the carrots from the pan; reserve until ready to serve.

Wash the asparagus well and snap off the tough stems. When close to serving time, bring about a cup of lightly salted water to boil in a sauté pan large enough to hold the asparagus in one layer. Add the asparagus to the pan, reduce the heat to a simmer, and cover the pan. Cook until the asparagus are just crisp-tender and bright green, from 1 to 3 minutes.

Remove the asparagus to an ice-water bath for about 5 minutes. Drain well and pat dry. When ready to serve, melt the butter in a sauté pan over medium heat. When the butter foams, add the asparagus and just heat through for a minute or two.

Arrange the vegetables on serving plates or a platter.

Seasons of the Vineyard
138

Rhubarb Meringue Tartlets with Strawberries

SERVES 8

In southern California's mild climate, there is little difference between late winter and early spring; fresh rhubarb and strawberries come to market in February. Sarah usually peels the rhubarb, but you may leave it unpeeled if you like the bright color and the texture, which has a little more body. If you like to work with a pastry bag, try some different shapes, such as squares or triangles. The meringues and curd may be made a day ahead. Store the meringues between wax or parchment paper in airtight containers. Chill the curd in an ice-water bath, then cover and store in the refrigerator.

Meringue Tartlets

- **4 LARGE EGG WHITES, AT ROOM TEMPERATURE**
- **¼ TEASPOON CREAM OF TARTAR**
- **PINCH SALT**
- **¾ CUP SUGAR**

Trace four 3-inch circles on each of two sheets of baking parchment. Reverse the parchment and place on baking sheets. If you will be making other shapes, trace outlines or pipe the meringues freehand. Preheat the oven to 175° F.

Beat the egg whites with the cream of tartar and salt until they hold soft peaks. Add the sugar, a tablespoon at a time, beating about 30 seconds after each addition. When all the sugar has been added, the meringue will be stiff and shiny.

Transfer the meringue to a pastry bag fitted with a large round or star tip and pipe out the base of the shells, following the shapes outlined on the parchment paper, or freehand. Build the shells by piping two layers of meringue on top of the bases.

Bake the meringues until they are completely dry and crisp, about 2 hours, changing the position of the baking sheets halfway through the baking. Cool to room temperature and store in airtight containers between layers of parchment or wax paper.

Rhubarb Curd

- **1 POUND RHUBARB, CLEANED, PEELED IF DESIRED, AND CHOPPED, ABOUT 3 CUPS**
- **JUICE AND CHOPPED ZEST OF 1 LEMON**
- **¾ CUP SUGAR**
- **¼ CUP WATER**
- **½ VANILLA BEAN, SPLIT LENGTHWISE**
- **6 TABLESPOONS UNSALTED BUTTER, CUT INTO BITS**
- **3 LARGE EGGS PLUS 2 LARGE YOLKS**

(continued)

Combine the rhubarb, lemon juice and zest, sugar, water, and vanilla in a nonreactive saucepan. Cover and cook over low heat until the rhubarb is completely soft, about 5 minutes. Uncover and cook until most of the liquid has evaporated and the pulp just begins to stick to the bottom of the pan, about 10 minutes. Remove the vanilla bean and puree the rhubarb in a food processor until completely smooth.

Measure 1½ cups of the puree and reserve the rest for another use. Place the measured puree in a nonreactive saucepan with the butter. Cook over low heat, stirring continually, until the butter is melted and incorporated into the puree.

Whisk the eggs and egg yolks together until just combined. Remove the rhubarb puree from the heat and whisk about ½ cup of it into the eggs. Add the egg mixture to the pan and continue whisking over low heat until the curd has thickened enough to coat the back of a spoon, from 7 to 10 minutes. Remove the curd to a bowl, whisking out any lumps, and cover with plastic wrap directly on the surface of the curd. Set the bowl into a larger bowl half filled with ice water and chill, stirring the curd occasionally. When cold, refrigerate.

ASSEMBLY

3 PINTS STRAWBERRIES

OPTIONAL: SUGAR OR LEMON JUICE

¼ CUP RED CURRANT OR APRICOT JELLY OR JAM

ZEST OF 1 LEMON, IN LONG STRANDS

FRESH MINT SPRIGS

Rinse the strawberries and trim the stems. Puree 2 pints of the berries in a food processor, adding a little sugar or lemon juice to balance the flavor.

Combine the jelly or jam and water in a small pan. Melt over low heat to make a glaze. Brush the remaining strawberries with the glaze and place them on a plate, blossom ends up.

Just before serving, divide the strawberry puree among 8 plates. Place a meringue shell in the center of each portion of puree. Spoon about 2 heaping tablespoons of the rhubarb curd in each shell and set the glazed strawberries on the curd. Garnish each tartlet with some strands of lemon zest and a mint sprig.

Art Reception at Wappo Hill

Gougères

Crudités with
Parsley-Yogurt Mayonnaise

Smithfield Ham

Raclette with Potatoes
and Cucumber and Onion Pickles

FUMÉ BLANC AND PINOT NOIR

The sculptures placed in and surrounding the Oakville winery's courtyard are one reflection of Robert's and Margrit's love of and commitment to the arts. Most visitors enjoy them, especially the children who climb on the Beniamino Bufano marble animals. The original architect's plan included an arch in the Vineyard Room, which Robert asked to be replaced with an atrium-style skylight so that the room could be an open exhibition space. Shortly after the winery opened, Robert started hosting art shows in the room. This program has continued and expanded to include theatrical performances and poetry readings, as well as classical concerts.

The Mondavi home on Wappo Hill, named for a native Napa tribe, was built with the spaciousness to accommodate more Bufano sculptures, and other art Robert and Margrit particularly love. Many of the pieces are folk art, collected on their travels. This setting naturally lends itself to the art receptions the Mondavis are happy to host. High among the good things in life for Robert and Margrit are the arts in their many forms. Robert has been working with others during the past several years to create a center for the arts, food, and wine in Napa. Margrit, as head of cultural affairs at the winery, keeps in touch with artists of all media from around the world, including many local artists.

hether they are hosting friends with the common purpose of furthering the arts, or any guests in their home, their first concern is to make people feel at ease and happy. For this late-afternoon reception, which brought together contributors to the de Young Museum in San Francisco, Margrit chose a menu that balanced the day and season. The raclette, warm from the fire, and the gougères, hot from the oven, warmed the guests on the cool, rainy day. The first spring vegetables were offered as crudités with a light mayonnaise. The Smithfield ham from Virginia was a treat for those who live in California. For the wines, Robert chose recent vintages of Fumé Blanc and Pinot Noir.

GOUGÈRES

Margrit learned to make gougères in Switzerland, where she grew up. Also, in the Burgundy region of France these little puffs are the perfect offering with wine. Pinot Noir is the natural, but they are also good with Fumé Blanc. Gougères are incomparable served about 5 minutes out of the oven, but are still quite enjoyable when they are made ahead. The dough can stand at cool (65° F) room temperature for several hours before being baked. The gougères can also be baked, cooled to room temperature, and then frozen for up to a month. Reheat them without thawing in a 325° F oven for about 15 minutes, until they are piping hot. The recipe is easily halved if you are serving fewer people.

2   CUPS MILK

2   TEASPOONS SALT

A SPRINKLE OF FRESH-GROUND PEPPER

8   TABLESPOONS UNSALTED BUTTER

2   CUPS UNBLEACHED ALL-PURPOSEFLOUR

8   LARGE EGGS, AT ROOM TEMPERATURE

8   OUNCES GRUYÈRE, EMMENTAL, OR ITALIAN FONTINA CHEESE, GRATED

1   LARGE EGG YOLK, BEATEN WITH 1 TABLESPOON WATER

Combine the milk, salt, and pepper in a large saucepan. Add the butter and bring the mixture to a boil. Remove the pan from the heat and add the flour all at once, stirring quickly and continually with a wooden spoon.

Return the pan to low heat, beating the mixture vigorously until it detaches from the sides of the pan, about 1 minute. Remove from the heat and cool for 5 minutes.

Beat the eggs, one at a time, into the mixture, incorporating as much as possible by moving the dough vigorously with the wooden spoon. When the dough is shiny and smooth, stir in the grated cheese. Cover the dough and let it cool until it is just warm.

Preheat the oven to 375° F and position a rack in the center of the oven. Lightly butter three or four baking sheets, or line them with parchment paper.

Form the dough into small mounds with teaspoons. Or, form into larger mounds with tablespoons. Push the mounds onto the prepared baking sheet. Brush lightly with the egg wash.

Bake for 15 minutes. Lower the heat to 350° F and bake for 15 to 20 minutes longer, until the gougères are a rich golden brown. Transfer to racks to cool for 5 minutes before serving warm.

CRUDITÉS WITH PARSLEY-YOGURT MAYONNAISE

Margrit says of this recipe, "Adding yogurt and parsley to mayonnaise lightens it and gives it a different flavor interest, as well. I like this especially with tender baby spring vegetables, like the little round carrots and mild radishes." Here use the nicest vegetables you can find—carrots, turnips, radishes, Belgian endive leaves, the first cherry tomatoes. The amounts of vegetables are easily doubled or halved if you are serving a different number of guests.

MAYONNAISE

1 LARGE EGG

ABOUT 2 TEASPOONS LEMON JUICE

SALT AND FRESH-GROUND PEPPER

¾ CUP OLIVE OIL, OR CANOLA OR OTHER MILD-FLAVORED OIL

½ CUP PLAIN YOGURT

¼ CUP MINCED FRESH ITALIAN PARSLEY LEAVES

Make the mayonnaise by adding the egg to a blender with a feed hole, or to a food processor. Add the lemon juice, a pinch of salt, and a few grindings of pepper and process.

Add ¼ cup of the oil, a few drops at a time, with the motor running. Add the remaining oil in a thin stream to emulsify the mayonnaise. When the mayonnaise has formed, stir in the yogurt and parsley. Adjust the seasoning with salt, pepper, or lemon juice. Refrigerate the mayonnaise, covered, until ready to serve.

VEGETABLES

1 POUND BABY CARROTS

1 POUND BABY TURNIPS

2 BUNCHES RADISHES

1 PINT TINY CHERRY TOMATOES

BELGIAN ENDIVES AND/OR SMALL LETTUCES FOR GARNISH

Scrub the carrots, turnips, and radishes well. Trim the tops, leaving some leaves for decoration and ease in dipping. Scrape or peel the skins from the carrots and turnips. Trim any long, thin roots from the vegetables. Wash the tomatoes and remove the stems. Core the Belgian endives and lettuces. Separate the leaves.

TO FINISH THE DISH

Arrange the vegetables decoratively on a platter. Place the mayonnaise in two small bowls and place the bowls on, or next to, the platter. Serve at cool room temperature.

Raclette with Potatoes and Cucumber and Onion Pickles

Margrit likes to serve the Swiss specialty of raclette cheese with the first tiny new potatoes of spring and with good pickles. When she doesn't have any of her own pickles, she buys good-quality cucumber and onion pickles in jars a day or two ahead and adds smashed garlic and a dried hot pepper for extra flavor. The recipe is easily expanded or cut down: calculate 2 ounces of cheese and three or four potatoes per person as part of an appetizer buffet. There is a special machine, a raclettière, to keep the cheese melting at an even rate, but for the best flavor, melt the cheese in an ovenproof dish before a wood fire (or, alternately, as far as possible from the oven broiler), and transfer the melted cheese to a plate over a heavy pan filled with boiling water. Place the pan on a heatproof surface on your buffet table. You can also use a fondue pot or hot plate to keep the cheese warm and slightly elastic.

12 OUNCES SOUR CUCUMBER PICKLES

12 OUNCES PICKLED ONIONS

4 GARLIC CLOVES, SMASHED AND PEELED

1 DRIED HOT PEPPER

2 POUNDS RACLETTE CHEESE

2 POUNDS MARBLE-SIZE NEW POTATOES

Cut the cucumber pickles into small bite-size pieces and place in a bowl with their liquid. Place the pickled onions in a bowl with their liquid. Divide the garlic between the cucumbers and onions and add the hot pepper to the cucumbers. Refrigerate for a day or two, then transfer to serving bowls to stand at room temperature at least an hour before serving.

Let the cheese stand at room temperature while you prepare the potatoes. Scrub the potatoes and place them in a pot; just cover with water. Cook the potatoes until they are just done, about 12 minutes. Drain the potatoes and place them in a serving dish.

When ready to serve, arrange the potatoes, cucumbers, and onions on a buffet table. Have ready forks, plates, and small knives to cut the cheese, so that guests can help themselves to the cheese, potatoes, and pickles.

Melt a layer of cheese as described above. Scrape the melted cheese onto a warm plate and place over a pot of boiling water, or on a hot plate, or in a fondue pot. Place the cheese next to the potatoes and pickles. Melt and replenish the cheese as necessary.

Celebrating Napa Valley Mustard

with Annie Roberts

Mustard Seed—Crusted Salmon
with Watercress Sauce

New Potatoes and Herbs in Parchment

CHARDONNAY

Spring Lettuce Salad
with Mustard-Fennel Vinaigrette

As chef at the winery, Annie plans menus according to the freshest seasonal ingredients she can find. Given the moderate climate of Napa and adjacent counties, Annie is blessed with abundance and variety in her daily food purchasing. It is the succession of different vegetables, fruits, herbs, fish, and cheeses that give her menus and dishes their characteristic taste of freshness and appropriateness. Annie's talent is to keep individual flavors clear while creating harmony and balance among all the ingredients.

When asked how she came to be a chef, Annie responded, "I grew up with good food. At home my mother always served simple, tasty dishes, based on lots of fresh vegetables and fruits. We traveled frequently in Europe, which made me want to learn to cook well in order to eat well. I've learned techniques from great chefs, here at the winery and in Europe, and this has been very helpful. Mainly, however, I like unfussy foods that don't take days and degrees and techniques to make. For me, the most important thing about food is an idea I share with my mother: Enjoying good food is a way of life rather than something to become a connoisseur of, to learn. And this is true of wine with food as well; pairing food and wine shouldn't be intimidating, but enjoyable."

nnie's mother, Margrit, has a story of when she discovered Annie's tendencies toward chefdom. "She was about one and a half years old when one day I came into the kitchen to find her on the floor with all the pots and pans around. She was tearing up pieces of newspaper and shifting them from pot to pan. I asked what she was doing and she replied, 'I'm making dinner for Snoopy,' who was our dog. I knew then that I had a chef on my hands."

or this menu, which Annie presented to a group of cooking professionals, she drew inspiration from the spring spectacle of mustard among the vines surrounding the winery. There is a month-long mustard festival in the Napa Valley, beginning in the southernmost town of Napa and continuing to the northernmost of Calistoga, following the billows of brilliant yellow bloom. The full-bodied Chardonnay Annie chose to serve stood up to the warmth and slight bite of mustard seed and oil.

MUSTARD SEED-CRUSTED FILLET OF SALMON SERVES 4

Annie Roberts designed this salmon dish to be served with the Watercress Sauce that follows, but the salmon is delicious without the sauce as well. If you don't have the mustard oil, use all canola oil. The recipe is easily doubled if you wish to serve more people.

¼ CUP MUSTARD SEEDS

½ CUP FRESH BREAD CRUMBS FROM FRENCH- OR ITALIAN-STYLE WHITE BREAD

1 TABLESPOON CHOPPED FRESH ITALIAN PARSLEY LEAVES

2 TEASPOONS CHOPPED FRESH THYME LEAVES

SALT AND FRESH-GROUND PEPPER

2 TABLESPOONS WHIPPING CREAM

1 LARGE EGG

1 POUND SALMON FILLET, SKINNED AND CUT CROSSWISE INTO 4 PORTIONS

1 TABLESPOON NAPA VALLEY MUSTARD-FLAVORED OIL

1 TABLESPOON CANOLA OIL

OPTIONAL: WATERCRESS SAUCE (RECIPE FOLLOWS)

Place the mustard seeds on a wooden cutting board and bear down on them with the bottom of a small skillet or pan, to break them slightly and release the oils. Mix them in a bowl with the bread crumbs, parsley, and thyme, and season well with salt and pepper.

In a second bowl, beat the cream and egg lightly together. Dip the skin side of each salmon piece in the egg and cream mixture, then in the crumb mixture. Place on a plate, crumb side up. The recipe may be done advance to this point; cover the plate loosely with wax paper and refrigerate.

Remove the fish from the refrigerator and let stand at room temperature for about 30 minutes before cooking. Preheat the oven to 375° F.

When ready to serve, heat the oil in a nonstick sauté pan over medium-high heat. Carefully place the fish pieces crumb side down, in the pan. Cook until rich golden brown, about 3 minutes.

Place the fish crust side up on a parchment paper–lined baking sheet. Bake until just done, about 4 minutes. The fish should have a rose-opaque center. Serve immediately, with the sauce, if desired.

This Watercress Sauce is quite versatile, enhancing full-flavored fish such as salmon and tuna, whether they are grilled, sautéed, poached, or baked. If you can't find the Napa Valley mustard-flavored oil, use olive oil instead, and add 1 teaspoon dry mustard to the food processor with the other ingredients. One trick Annie uses to help emulsify a simple vinegar and oil sauce such as this one is to measure the oils into the same measuring cup, then refrigerate them for one to several hours. Leftover sauce is good as a dressing for cooked vegetables and salads, and with hard-cooked eggs.

3 TABLESPOONS CHAMPAGNE VINEGAR OR WHITE WINE VINEGAR

3 TABLESPOONS RICE VINEGAR

1 BUNCH GREEN ONIONS, CHOPPED WITH SOME GREEN, ABOUT ¾ CUP

1½ CUPS WATERCRESS LEAVES

½ CUP NAPA VALLEY MUSTARD-FLAVORED OIL

½ CUP SAFFLOWER OR CANOLA OIL

SALT AND FRESH-GROUND PEPPER

OPTIONAL: LEMON JUICE TO TASTE

Combine the vinegars, green onions, and watercress in a food processor and process until quite fine, stopping to scrape down the workbowl two or three times.

Add the oils in a fine stream until they are used up and the sauce has emulsified. Season with salt and pepper and adjust, if you like, with lemon juice. Transfer to a serving dish, cover, and keep refrigerated until ready to serve.

New Potatoes and Herbs in Parchment SERVES 4

New potatoes of different colors—red, purple, yellow, white—are sometimes available; the color cooks out a bit, but the flavors are distinct. The important thing in parchment cooking is to choose ingredients of the same size and cut them the same thickness. For this dish, potatoes about 1½ inches in diameter work well.

1 POUND NEW POTATOES

4 PIECES PARCHMENT PAPER, EACH ABOUT 15 INCHES SQUARE

3 FRESH THYME SPRIGS, LEAVES MINCED

3 FRESH ITALIAN PARSLEY SPRIGS, LEAVES MINCED

3 LARGE GARLIC CLOVES, SLICED VERY THIN

2 TABLESPOONS EXTRA-VIRGIN OLIVE OIL

SALT AND FRESH-GROUND PEPPER

Preheat the oven to 400° F.

Scrub potatoes well and cut about ¼-inch thick. Divide the potatoes equally among the parchment pieces, arranging them on one side. Sprinkle the herbs over the potatoes; scatter the garlic slices over. Drizzle the potatoes with the olive oil and salt and pepper well.

Fold the other side of the parchment over each portion of potatoes and trim to a semicircle shape. Crimp the edges of the parchment well. Place the packages on two baking sheets and place in the oven. Bake the potatoes for 18 to 20 minutes; changing the position of the baking sheets halfway through the baking. Open the packages with scissors or a sharp knife and place on serving plates next to your main course. Serve immediately.

Spring Lettuce Salad
with Mustard-Fennel Vinaigrette

The mustard oil gives the vinaigrette a pleasant bite. If you can't find the mustard oil, use canola oil and ½ teaspoon mustard powder, or to taste. A full-flavored range of greens and herbs is best with the vinaigrette, which is also good with cooked vegetable salads of asparagus, beets, broccoli, carrots, or cauliflower.

½ CUP GRATED FENNEL BULB

⅓ CUP NAPA VALLEY MUSTARD-FLAVORED OIL

1 ½ TABLESPOONS WHITE WINE VINEGAR

1 SHALLOT, MINCED

2 TABLESPOONS MINCED FENNEL LEAVES

SALT AND FRESH-GROUND PEPPER

1 QUART MIXED FIELD OR BABY GREENS AND LETTUCES

GARNISH: MUSTARD OR NASTURTIUM BLOSSOMS

Combine the grated fennel and mustard-flavored oil in a small nonreactive saucepan. Simmer the mixture with bubbles just breaking the surface for 15 minutes. Cool the mixture to room temperature, then puree in a blender or food processor. Strain the puree.

Combine the vinegar, shallot, and fennel leaves in a bowl. Whisk in the puree to form an emulsion. Season with salt and pepper.

Wash the greens and dry them well. Keep covered in the refrigerator until ready to dress.

When ready to serve the salad, taste the vinaigrette and adjust the seasoning. Toss the salad with about half of the vinaigrette; adding more vinaigrette if necessary. Garnish the salad with mustard or nasturtium blossoms and serve immediately.

SPRING RECIPES

ARTICHOKES WITH JALAPEÑO MAYONNAISE

According to Margrit, "Artichokes are the most beautiful and best-tasting in the spring. I like to serve them as a first course, arranged like flowers on individual plates; most often I choose rather simple plates, as the artichokes are so decorative."

The artichokes may be steamed early in the day, and are best served at cool room temperature.

6 TO 8 MEDIUM-SIZE ARTICHOKES

1 LEMON, HALVED

1 LARGE EGG

JUICE OF ½ LEMON

¼ TEASPOON SALT

FRESH-GROUND PEPPER

½ TEASPOON BALSAMIC VINEGAR

1 JALAPEÑO PEPPER, STEMMED, SEEDED, AND MINCED

¾ CUP OLIVE OIL

Trim the artichokes of stems, tough outer leaves, and thorns, rubbing with a cut lemon as you trim. When you have finished trimming the artichokes, slice the lemon and add it, with water enough to steam, to the bottom of a vegetable steamer.

Place the artichokes in the top of the steamer and cook them until a knife just pierces the bottoms, about 15 minutes. Remove the artichokes to a platter to cool.

Make the mayonnaise by adding the egg to a blender with a feed hole, or to a food processor. Add the lemon juice, salt, a few grindings of pepper, the balsamic vinegar, and jalapeño pepper.

Add ¼ cup of the olive oil, a few drops at a time, with the motor running. Add the remaining olive oil in a thin stream to emulsify the mayonnaise. When the mayonnaise is ready, adjust the seasoning with salt, pepper, lemon juice, or balsamic vinegar. Refrigerate the mayonnaise, covered, until ready to serve.

When ready to serve, pull the leaves from the artichokes and remove the chokes. Arrange each artichoke on a serving plate like a flower, with the heart in the center. Place about 2 tablespoons of the mayonnaise in the hearts, or on the side of the plates. Pass the remaining mayonnaise.

MINESTRONE

Minestrone can be made in any season, but is most traditionally Italian in late winter and spring, when the first-of-season vegetables become available. The recipe below was one of Rosa Mondavi's, as transcribed by her daughter Helen and granddaughter Serena. Balance was one of Rosa's key ideas in cooking. Helen says, "My mother's minestrone was about two-thirds broth and one-third other ingredients and it was very important to get the balance right, since we ate the soup as a first course. Mother would use different vegetables, according to what was best at the time."

2 OUNCES SALT PORK, MINCED

1 ONION, DICED

2 CARROTS, PEELED AND DICED

1 CELERY STALK, DICED

3 QUARTS CHICKEN BROTH

4 OUNCES GREEN BEANS, CUT IN 1-INCH PIECES

8 OUNCES SAVOY CABBAGE, CUT IN ABOUT 1-INCH
PIECES

12 OUNCES FRESH PEAS, SHELLED, OR SWISS CHARD,
LEAVES SHREDDED AND STEMS TRIMMED AND
DICED

2 SMALL ZUCCHINI, ABOUT 4 OUNCES EACH,
QUARTERED AND CUT IN ¼-INCH PIECES

2 FRESH TOMATOES, ABOUT 6 OUNCES EACH,
PEELED, SEEDED, AND DICED, OR ONE 14-OUNCE
CAN DICED TOMATOES

4 OUNCES SMALL SHELL OR TUBE PASTA

SALT AND FRESH-GROUND PEPPER

½ CUP CHOPPED FRESH ITALIAN PARSLEY

2 GARLIC CLOVES, MINCED

⅓ CUP EXTRA-VIRGIN OLIVE OIL

⅔ CUP FRESH-GRATED PARMESAN CHEESE

Render the salt pork in a soup pot over low heat for about 10 minutes. Add the onion, carrots, and celery and sweat the vegetables, covered, until softened, about 10 minutes.

Add the broth and simmer for about 15 minutes. Add the green beans and cabbage and simmer for 5 minutes. Add the peas or chard and simmer for 5 minutes. Add the zucchini, tomatoes, and pasta and simmer for 10 minutes. Season the soup with salt and pepper to taste.

Just before serving, mix the parsley, garlic, olive oil, and Parmesan together in a bowl. Ladle the soup into serving bowls and add a spoonful of the parsley-cheese mixture to each serving. Serve hot.

WATERCRESS SOUP

SERVES 6

Margrit says, "This soup is one of my light picnic recipes because I think we enjoy food most when it is full of flavor but not of calories, especially when we are eating outdoors. For my taste, the soup is best cold at a picnic, though I also serve it hot before dinner."

4 CUPS CHICKEN BROTH

1 GARLIC CLOVE

BOUQUET GARNI: 3 FRESH ITALIAN PARSLEY SPRIGS
AND 2 FRESH THYME SPRIGS, TIED TOGETHER

1 BUNCH WATERCRESS, ABOUT 6 OUNCES, LARGE
STEMS REMOVED

1 GREEN ONION CHOPPED FINE WITH SOME GREEN

SALT AND FRESH-GROUND PEPPER

ABOUT ⅓ CUP YOGURT

Combine the chicken broth in a saucepan with the garlic clove and bouquet garni. Bring the broth almost to a boil. Meanwhile, reserve 6 watercress sprigs for garnish.

Remove the garlic and bouquet garni from the broth, and add the watercress and green onion. Cook the soup at a simmer for 5 minutes. Pass the soup through a food mill, or puree in batches in a blender or food processor.

Adjust the seasoning with salt and pepper. Serve hot or cold, with a dollop of yogurt and a watercress sprig to garnish each serving.

CHEVRIGNON SHRIMP AND PASTA

Sarah Scott created this very Italian pasta dish—light and flavorful, with just enough sauce to coat the pasta—to highlight the well-balanced fruit and acid of Chevrignon, a blend of Sauvignon Blanc and Semillon grapes.

1   POUND IMPORTED PENNE PASTA
2   TABLESPOONS OLIVE OIL
SALT AND FRESH-GROUND PEPPER
1   POUND MEDIUM SHRIMP, SHELLED AND DEVEINED
1-INCH PIECE FRESH GINGERROOT, GRATED OR MINCED
4   GREEN ONIONS, MINCED WITH ABOUT 4 INCHES OF GREEN
1   RIPE TOMATO, ABOUT 6 OUNCES, DICED FINE
½   CUP FISH STOCK OR BOTTLED CLAM JUICE
½   CUP CHEVRIGNON OR OTHER DRY WHITE WINE
⅓   CUP WHIPPING CREAM
JUICE OF 1 LEMON, OR TO TASTE
GARNISH: CHOPPED FRESH ITALIAN PARSLEY

Cook the penne in abundant boiling salted water until al dente, 8 to 12 minutes. Drain the pasta and toss it with 1 tablespoon of the oil. Season lightly with salt and pepper and set aside.

In a sauté pan large enough to hold the pasta and shrimp, heat the remaining oil over medium heat. Add the shrimp and just cook through, 2 to 3 minutes. Remove the shrimp to a plate.

Add the gingerroot and green onions to the sauté pan. Cook over medium heat until the gingerroot is slightly browned and the onions are soft. Add the tomato, fish stock or clam juice, and the wine. Cook over high heat until the liquid is reduced by half. Add the cream and cook for a minute or two, until the sauce is slightly thickened.

Return the shrimp to the pan and add the pasta. Stir to coat well and remove from the heat. Add lemon juice to taste, and adjust the seasoning with salt and pepper. Turn onto a serving platter and sprinkle with chopped parsley.

SALAD OF FOIE GRAS AND HARICOTS VERTS

Margrit was inspired to make this salad when Robert brought her a lovely foie gras from one of his trips to New York. The first spring haricots verts were just in the market, which gave Margrit the idea to contrast their fresh vegetable flavor and texture with the rich, unctuous quality of foie gras.

To make the dish several hours ahead, cook the haricots verts and refrigerate them. Make the vinaigrette and keep it in a cool place, or refrigerate. Have the hazelnuts and baguette ready. Once the foie gras is cut, the salad should be assembled within 30 minutes or so. For ease in cutting, the foie gras should be well chilled. Holding the knife blade above the steam from a tea kettle works as well as rinsing, and is a bit quicker.

French Sauternes is the classic wine with foie gras; a Fumé Blanc or Johannisberg Riesling Botrytis would also be good. Lacking these, Champagne or méthode champenoise sparkling wine, or a full-flavored Fumé Blanc would work well with this salad.

Cut the foie gras into ½-inch dice with a thin-bladed knife, rinsing the knife in hot water after each slice. Cover and refrigerate.

Bring several quarts of water to a boil and salt lightly. Add the haricots verts and cook until just crisp-tender, about 3 minutes. Drain the beans and immediately plunge them in a bowl of ice water to maintain their color. Drain the beans and dry on paper towels.

Add the sherry vinegar to a small bowl. Whisk in the hazelnut oil. Season well with lemon juice, salt, and pepper.

Gently toss the foie gras in a bowl with the haricots verts, vinaigrette, and hazelnuts. Serve immediately on cool plates or a platter and pass the baguette.

8   OUNCES FRESH TERRINE OF FOIE GRAS, WELL
    CHILLED

1   POUND HARICOTS VERTS, ALSO SOLD AS SMALL
    FRENCH GREEN BEANS

2   TABLESPOONS SHERRY VINEGAR

¼   CUP HAZELNUT OIL

    LEMON JUICE

    SALT AND FRESH-GROUND PEPPER

⅓   CUP HAZELNUTS, LIGHTLY TOASTED (PAGE 120),
    SKINS RUBBED OFF AND NUTS HALVED

1 CRUSTY BAGUETTE, SLICED, TOASTED IF DESIRED

MARC MENEAU'S SQUAB CONTI WITH CRESS

Marc Meneau is chef d'honneur at the three-star restaurant L'Esperance, in Saint Père Sous Vezelay, France. This elegant and delicious dish of his requires some advance planning. Begin the day before, with soaking the boned squab in some cream. Make the sauce base and watercress as described below.

If you have your butcher bone the breasts and remove the thigh bones, be sure that he gives you the carcasses for a stock that will enhance any number of dishes from simple risotto, mashed potatoes, or chicken braise, to squab consommé or sauces for squab, duck, or quail dishes. Make the stock by roasting the carcasses with a quartered onion and carrot in a hot oven until well-browned. Transfer the bones and vegetables to a stockpot and deglaze the roasting pan with water. Just cover the bones with the deglazing juices and water and add some parsley and thyme, if you like. Remove any fat and refrigerate for four to five days, or freeze for up to two months.

    6   SQUAB, BREASTS AND THIGHS BONED
1 ½   CUPS WHIPPING CREAM
    3   TABLESPOONS CHOPPED SHALLOTS
    3   TABLESPOONS UNSALTED BUTTER
    4   TABLESPOONS MADEIRA
    5   TABLESPOONS CHOPPED WHITE ONION
  ½   TEASPOON DIJON MUSTARD
    1   POUND WATERCRESS, WASHED AND LARGE STEMS
        REMOVED
    ABOUT 2 TEASPOONS LEMON JUICE
    SALT AND FRESH-GROUND PEPPER

Salt and pepper the breasts and thighs lightly. Place them in a dish that just holds them and cover with ½ cup of the cream. Cover with plastic wrap and refrigerate overnight.

Make the sauce base by placing the shallots and 2 tablespoons of the butter in a nonreactive saucepan over low heat and cooking for 5 minutes, stirring frequently. Pour off the fat, return the pan to the heat, add the Madeira, and reduce over low heat to a glaze. Add the onion and ½ cup cream. Cook for about 7 minutes over low heat to reduce by half.

Off the heat, stir in the mustard. Let the sauce base cool at room temperature, then place in a blender and puree. Refrigerate the sauce base.

Reserve 8 watercress sprigs. Blanch the remaining watercress for 2 seconds. Drain and refresh in ice water. Puree the blanced watercress, with the water that clings to its leaves, in a blender; you should have about ¾ cup watercress puree.

The next day, remove the squab and the sauce base from the refrigerator about 1 ½ hours before cooking them.

When ready to finish the dish, whip the remaining cream to soft peaks. Preheat the oven broiler.

Transfer the squab and the cream that clings to them to an ovenproof pan. Cook them about 5 inches from the broiler, with the oven door ajar, until the breasts are medium-rare, and the thighs are well-done, 3 to 4 minutes on each side for the breasts, 6 to 7 minutes on each side for the thighs. When the squab is cooked, wrap it loosely in foil and set aside to rest.

Heat the sauce thoroughly over low heat without letting it boil. Stir in the watercress puree and whipped cream and heat gently. Stir in about 2 teaspoons of lemon juice and correct the seasoning with salt, pepper, and more lemon juice, if necessary.

To serve, heat the reserved watercress sprigs in the remaining tablespoon of butter over high heat; remove from the heat when the watercress is bright green. Cut the squab breasts horizontally into two slices each.

Arrange two thighs on the tops of serving plates. Place about ¼ cup of the sauce in the center of each plate. Fan the breast meat below the sauce. Garnish the thighs with the watercress sprigs and serve immediately.

RACK OF LAMB WITH HERB CRUST SERVES 6

You can make this special main course for dinner even on a working day, as Margrit does. Order the lamb the day before and ask your butcher to french cut the racks: to crack the vertebrae between the ribs, peel back the rough upper layer of the meat and fat, leaving it attached, and trim the excess fat that lies on the ribs. For the best flavor, buy local or United States lamb, rather than imported.

2 RACKS OF LAMB, 7 TO 8 RIBS PER RACK, ABOUT 5 POUNDS AFTER TRIMMING

LEAVES FROM 8 TO 10 FRESH ITALIAN PARSLEY SPRIGS

LEAVES FROM 4 TO 5 FRESH BASIL SPRIGS, OR 2 TEASPOONS DRIED BASIL

3 GARLIC CLOVES, MINCED

1 TEASPOON KOSHER SALT

Peel back the rough upper layers of the racks; if your butcher has not trimmed the excess fat that lies on the ribs, trim it carefully.

Chop the parsley and basil leaves fine and mix them with the garlic and salt. Pat the herb mixture on the ribs of the racks and cover with the upper layers. Place the racks in a shallow roasting pan or rimmed baking sheet, bones facing each other in the center of the pan. Refrigerate 3 hours, or up to 8 hours. Remove the racks from the refrigerator 2 hours before roasting.

When ready to roast the lamb, preheat the oven to 450° F. Place the lamb in the center of the oven and roast for 20 to 25 minutes for rare to medium-rare lamb.

Remove the lamb from the oven and let stand 10 minutes before carving. Before serving, remove the rough upper layer, if desired. To carve, slice the ribs between the bones.

Dorothy Mondavi's Grilled Chicken Breasts with Mixed Green Salad

Since Dorothy helps at the Mondavi winery as well as caring for five children, she often cooks simple, delicious one-dish family meals, like this one, that please both children and adults. She also serves this in the winter over risotto, such as the one on page 117. About an hour is ideal for marinating the chicken, but when Dorothy is short of time, or needs to wait before cooking the chicken, she has found that a little less or more time doesn't change the dish. The recipe is easily doubled for a larger group of people, and makes a fine picnic salad if you pack the chicken, lettuce, and vinaigrette separately and keep them chilled until shortly before serving. Serve the salad with crusty bread and Pinot Noir or any wine you like with chicken for an easy alfresco lunch or dinner.

Chicken and Marinade

- 4 BONELESS, SKINLESS WHOLE CHICKEN BREASTS
- 1½ TO 2 TABLESPOONS EXTRA-VIRGIN OLIVE OIL
- 2 GARLIC CLOVES
- 1 LARGE OR 2 SMALL LEMONS
- SALT AND FRESH-GROUND PEPPER
- ABOUT ⅓ CUP CHOPPED FRESH CILANTRO

Rub the chicken breasts well all over with the olive oil. Press the garlic onto the chicken breasts and rub all over. Squeeze the lemon juice over the chicken and toss well. Marinate, covered, at cool room temperature for 30 minutes to 2 hours.

Prepare a medium-hot grill, or preheat the oven broiler. Grill the chicken until it is just cooked through, 3 to 4 minutes on each side. If you are broiling the chicken, place it on a rack in a broiler pan about 5 inches from the heat. Cook until the chicken is just done, 3 to 4 minutes on a side.

Remove the chicken to a platter to cool about 5 minutes before cutting into diagonal slices about ¼ inch thick. Season with salt and pepper and toss with the chopped cilantro.

Salad and Vinaigrette

- 1½ QUARTS GARDEN LETTUCES AND HERBS, OR FARMERS' MARKET OR SUPERMARKET BABY LETTUCE MIX
- 2 TABLESPOONS RED WINE VINEGAR
- ¼ CUP EXTRA-VIRGIN OLIVE OIL
- SALT AND FRESH-GROUND PEPPER
- 1 PINT CHERRY TOMATOES

Clean the lettuces and dry them. Add the vinegar to a small bowl or measuring cup and whisk in the olive oil. Season with salt and pepper. Wash and halve the cherry tomatoes. Toss the vinaigrette with salad and place on a platter. Arrange the chicken and cherry tomatoes on top and serve.

FELICIA SORENSON'S HOT PINEAPPLE CURRY

Felicia Sorenson lives in Hong Kong, where she is a cookbook author, restaurant consultant, and cooking teacher. She demonstrated many dishes of intricate Asian flavors at the winery's Great Chefs program and illustrated how spicy and hot foods can be enjoyed with wine. This curry is rather thick, moderately hot (though that depends on the heat of the chilies you use), and makes a wonderful accompaniment to simple grills of fish, chicken, pork, or lamb. With the curry Felicia served lamb and chicken and chose a Cabernet Sauvignon. The vegetable curry powder is a blend of the sweet, citrus, and warm flavors of coriander, cumin, and fennel seeds. It can enliven many vegetables, especially root crops and greens.

VEGETABLE CURRY POWDER

- 3 TABLESPOONS CORIANDER SEEDS
- 3 TABLESPOONS CUMIN SEEDS
- 1½ TABLESPOONS FENNEL SEEDS

Grind the seeds separately in a spice grinder or clean coffee mill. Mix the ground seeds and grind again to a fine powder. Store the powder in a glass jar with a tight-fitting lid, away from heat and light.

PINEAPPLE CURRY

- 2 POUNDS PINEAPPLE
- 3 TABLESPOONS VEGETABLE OIL, SUCH AS PEANUT OR CANOLA
- 6 CURRY LEAVES, IF AVAILABLE
- ½-INCH PIECE GINGERROOT, PEELED AND MINCED OR GRATED
- 3 GARLIC CLOVES, MINCED
- 1 ONION, DICED FINE
- 1 FRESH RED CHILI, SUCH AS SERRANO, SLICED THIN
- 1 FRESH GREEN CHILI, SUCH AS JALAPEÑO OR SERRANO, SLICED THIN
- 2 TABLESPOONS VEGETABLE CURRY POWDER (SEE ABOVE)
- 1 TABLESPOON CHILI POWDER
- ½ TEASPOON TURMERIC
- 1 TEASPOON MUSTARD POWDER
- 2-INCH PIECE CINNAMON STICK
- 1 TEASPOON SUGAR
- 1½ TEASPOONS SALT
- 1 CUP CANNED UNSWEETENED COCONUT MILK

Peel the pineapple, core it, and cut into ½-inch cubes. Reserve.

Heat the oil in a large nonreactive sauté pan over medium heat and add the curry leaves, gingerroot, garlic, and onion. Stir well and cook for 2 minutes.

Add the pineapple, red and green chilies, vegetable curry powder, chili powder, turmeric, mustard powder, cinnamon, sugar, and salt. Mix the ingredients well and cook for 10 minutes.

Add the coconut milk and bring gently to a boil. Reduce the heat to a simmer and cook for 5 to 10 minutes, until the flavors have melded. Serve hot.

Yellow Rice (Kaha Bath)

Felicia Sorenson's lively food shows the influences of the many cuisines of Hong Kong. It is flavorful yet not overpowering, with the spices and herbs creating a whole greater than the parts. Serve this fragrant rice with grilled fish, chicken, or vegetable curries such as the preceding Pineapple Curry. The rice is delicious with Pinot Noir or, depending on the main courses, with a young Cabernet Sauvignon.

- **2 CUPS BASMATI OR GOOD-QUALITY LONG-GRAIN RICE**
- **2 TABLESPOONS GHEE OR CLARIFIED BUTTER**
- **6 SHALLOTS, SLICED THIN**
- **6 CARDAMOM PODS, SEEDS REMOVED FROM PODS**
- **6 WHOLE CLOVES**
- **6 PEPPERCORNS**
- **1 TEASPOON TURMERIC**
- **2-INCH PIECE LEMON GRASS**
- **2-INCH PIECE CINNAMON STICK**
- **2 TEASPOONS SALT**
- **2½ CUPS CHICKEN BROTH**
- **1 CUP CANNED UNSWEETENED COCONUT MILK**

Wash the rice until the water runs clear. Drain and set aside.

Heat the ghee in a large saucepan over medium heat. Add the shallots and fry until they are transparent, about 5 minutes.

Add the spices, salt, and rice. Cook, stirring continuously for 2 or 3 minutes. Add the chicken broth and coconut milk. Cover and bring to a boil. Reduce the heat immediately to a simmer and cook, covered, until the liquid has been absorbed, about 20 minutes.

Let the rice stand, covered, off the heat for about 5 minutes. Remove the spices from the top of the rice and fluff the rice lightly with a fork. Transfer to a warm serving dish and serve hot.

SALMON SALAD

This is another of Margrit's light picnic dishes, where the fish and greens are balanced in quantity, and the flavors highlighted by a vinaigrette with many tastes. She also serves the salad as a first course before dinners. It is best served right after it is assembled, though the salmon and vinaigrette may be prepared a few hours ahead and kept in the refrigerator.

1 ½ POUNDS SALMON FILLET, SKIN REMOVED
     SALT AND FRESH-GROUND PEPPER
     ABOUT ¼ CUP EXTRA-VIRGIN OLIVE OIL
½   TEASPOON LEMON JUICE
½   TEASPOON BALSAMIC VINEGAR
½   TEASPOON SHERRY VINEGAR
1 ½ TEASPOONS RED WINE, SUCH AS CABERNET
     SAUVIGNON
1   SHALLOT, MINCED
1   HEAD ESCAROLE, ABOUT 8 OUNCES, OR AN EQUAL
     AMOUNT OF MIXED BABY LETTUCES, TRIMMED,
     CLEANED, AND DRIED
     OPTIONAL GARNISHES: CHIVE, NASTURTIUM, OR
     ARUGULA BLOSSOMS

Slice the salmon about ¼ inch thick on a diagonal and salt and pepper lightly. Add about ½ tablespoon of the olive oil to a nonstick sauté pan large enough to hold the salmon without crowding. Cook the salmon in batches if necessary.

Place the pan over medium heat. When the oil just shimmers, add the salmon and cook for about 30 seconds on each side. As the salmon is done, remove it to a platter.

Combine the lemon juice, balsamic vinegar, sherry vinegar, red wine, and shallot in a bowl. Whisk in the remaining olive oil to form an emulsion. Adjust the seasoning with salt and pepper, and more vinegar or wine if necessary.

Toss the escarole with about half the vinaigrette and arrange on a platter or plates. Arrange the salmon slices on top and drizzle it with the remaining vinaigrette. Garnish the salad with edible flowers, if desired.

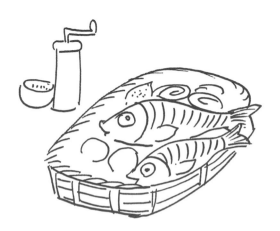

Asparagus with Sun-Dried Tomato Vinaigrette

This pretty and tasty salad is one of Annie Roberts's favorite dishes for entertaining, as it can be made early on the day it is served. When asparagus are pencil thin, they may be snapped at the point where the stems become tough. If you are lucky enough to find large asparagus, choose spears of about equal size so that they cook evenly. Snap off the tough stems, and using a vegetable peeler or a thin, sharp knife, peel about 3 inches of the tender stems for even cooking and a nice color contrast.

3 POUNDS ASPARAGUS, TOUGH ENDS TRIMMED AND STALKS PEELED IF NECESSARY

½ CUP SUN-DRIED TOMATOES IN OIL, DRAINED AND CHOPPED FINE

2 TABLESPOONS BALSAMIC VINEGAR

2 TABLESPOONS LEMON ZEST, IN LONG SHREDS

2 SHALLOTS, CHOPPED

¼ CUP CAPERS, RINSED AND CHOPPED

¼ CUP CHOPPED FRESH ITALIAN PARSLEY

ABOUT ⅓ CUP OLIVE OIL

SALT AND FRESH-GROUND PEPPER

Blanch the asparagus in boiling water until crisp-tender. Drain and refresh immediately in ice water. Drain again and pat the asparagus dry with kitchen towels.

Place the sun-dried tomatoes in a small bowl and add the balsamic vinegar. Mince about two thirds of the lemon zest and reserve the rest for garnish. Add the minced lemon zest, shallots, capers, and parsley to the tomatoes. Whisk in the olive oil to make an emulsion.

Taste the vinaigrette and adjust the seasoning with salt, pepper, and more olive oil, if desired. Pour the vinaigrette over the asparagus and garnish with the remaining lemon zest. Serve at cool room temperature. If you make the salad ahead, cover and refrigerate. Remove from the refrigerator an hour or so before serving.

MARGRIT'S RHUBARB PIE

"Rhubarb is in season in California beginning in late winter and continuing through spring," observes Margrit. "I suggest that everyone take advantage of the special tart flavor of fresh rhubarb. This is a rather rich pie, therefore a small slice will do, but don't be surprised if your family or friends ask for seconds. For a fine finish to a spring meal, serve the pie with whole strawberries and Moscato d'Oro. If you make the dough just before the pie, you needn't wash out the food processor bowl; a crumb of pie dough won't hurt the filling."

You will need half of the pastry dough for this recipe; freeze the remaining portion for another tart or pie.

PASTRY DOUGH (PAGE 193)
1 ½ **POUNDS RHUBARB**
3 **LARGE EGGS**
1 **CUP WHIPPING CREAM**
⅔ **CUP BROWN SUGAR, PACKED**
PINCH SALT
OPTIONAL GARNISH: WHOLE STRAWBERRIES

Divide the pastry dough in half and roll one portion to fit a 9- or 9½-inch pie plate and chill it in the freezer for at least 15 minutes; reserve the other portion for another use. Preheat the oven to 400° F.

Peel away the thin outer layer of rhubarb and cut the rhubarb into 1-inch pieces. Set aside. Place the eggs, cream, brown sugar, and salt in a food processor and mix together for about 1 minute.

Remove the pie plate from the freezer and fill it with the rhubarb. Pour the custard mixture over. Bake the pie for 10 minutes, then reduce the heat to 375° F. Bake until the custard is set and a knife comes clean when inserted in the center, about 35 minutes longer.

Cool the pie on a rack and serve, garnished if desired with strawberries, at room temperature. Or, after the pie is at room temperature, refrigerate it for up to 4 hours, and serve it slightly chilled.

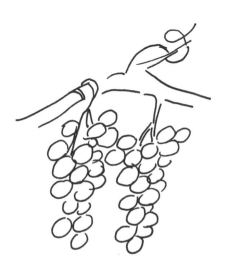

TROISGROS FROISSES (CRUMPLED COOKIES)

These unusual cookies from Pierre and Michel Troisgros are delicious and fun to serve with ice cream. To make them, you will need nonstick muffin-top pans. If you have three or four pans in the oven at the same time, watch the cookies carefully, and adjust the position of the pans so the cookies bake evenly. It is helpful to have someone to work with you to crumple the cookies when they come from the oven; be careful not to burn your fingers. The cookies may be made a day ahead and stored between wax paper in airtight tins. Just before serving, place the cookies on a baking sheet and crisp them in a preheated 300° F oven for 10 minutes.

If you aren't serving the froisses with ice cream, counterpoint their delicate texture with caramel lace. Melt ½ cup sugar with 2 tablespoons water and 2 tablespoons light Karo syrup in a small saucepan over medium heat. When the caramel is pale gold, drizzle threads of it with a fork into small free-form shapes onto a well-buttered baking sheet. When the caramel is cool, remove it carefully and place the pieces between sheets of wax paper in airtight tins.

Preheat the oven to 350° F. Very lightly butter the molds of two nonstick muffin-top pans.

Combine the sugar, flour, egg whites, vanilla, and salt in a bowl. Whisk vigorously to mix the ingredients thoroughly, about 30 seconds. Add the melted butter and the warm water and whisk together well.

Pour a scant tablespoon of the batter into each mold of the prepared muffin-top pans. Place the pans in the oven and bake for 4 minutes. Rotate the position of the pans and bake another 4 to 6 minutes.

The cookies are done when the edges have browned about ¼ inch and the centers are set. Remove the pans from the oven, and carefully crumple the cookies, pinching them in the center. Place the crumpled cookies on a platter to cool completely.

When the cookies are cool, arrange them on a platter in a cone shape. Surround with caramel lace (see note above), if desired.

½ CUP SUGAR

¼ CUP UNBLEACHED ALL-PURPOSE FLOUR

3 LARGE EGG WHITES

½ TEASPOON PURE VANILLA EXTRACT

PINCH SALT

2 TABLESPOONS UNSALTED BUTTER, MELTED

2 CUPS WARM WATER

ROSA MONDAVI'S HERMIT COOKIES

These quintessential kid-pleasing cookies are well remembered by Serena Ventura Chickering, one of Rosa's granddaughters, who collected many of her grandmother's recipes by watching her make dishes, then transcribing the approximate amounts of the ingredients and the procedures. Serena recalls that "Nonna didn't cook from recipes, even when baking. She knew when the dough or batter was right by the look and feel of it."

8	TABLESPOONS UNSALTED BUTTER, SOFTENED
1½	CUPS LIGHT BROWN SUGAR, PACKED
2	LARGE EGGS, LIGHTLY BEATEN
2	TABLESPOONS BUTTERMILK
3	CUPS UNBLEACHED ALL-PURPOSE FLOUR
½	TEASPOON BAKING SODA
1	TABLESPOON BAKING POWDER
½	TEASPOON FRESH-GRATED NUTMEG
½	TEASPOON GROUND CINNAMON
1	CUP WALNUTS, CHOPPED COARSE

Preheat the oven to 350° F. Butter and flour two baking sheets, or line them with parchment paper.

Beat the butter in a large bowl with an electric mixer. Add the sugar and beat until the mixture is very light and fluffy. Add the eggs and buttermilk and beat well together.

Sift the flour with the baking soda, baking powder, nutmeg, and cinnamon. Toss the walnuts in about a cup of the sifted ingredients. Stir the flour mixture, in two batches, into the butter mixture, mixing well to combine. Stir in the walnuts and remaining flour mixture.

Using two teaspoons, place the cookie dough by the heaping teaspoonful onto the prepared baking sheets, about 1½ inches apart. Bake on the center oven shelves for 10 to 12 minutes, changing the position of the baking sheets halfway through the baking. The tops of the cookies are pale golden brown when they are done.

Remove the cookies to racks to cool. Store in airtight tins for up to a week.

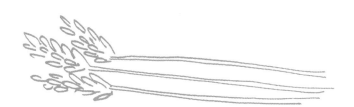

ANNIE ROBERTS'S STRAWBERRY-WALNUT WAFERS

These melt-in-your-mouth refrigerator cookies combine the tart-sweet flavor of strawberries with the crunchiness and nuttiness of walnuts. They are best eaten on the day they are made, but the wafers can be baked ahead, stored in airtight tins, and glazed and garnished before serving. A little Moscato d'Oro finishes the glaze, making the wine a wonderful match with the cookies. If you don't have Moscato d'Oro, use another slightly sweet wine, such as a late harvest Johannisberg Riesling.

COOKIES

- 1 CUP (8 OUNCES) UNSALTED BUTTER, SOFTENED
- 2 TABLESPOONS WALNUT OIL
- ½ CUP GRANULATED SUGAR
- ¼ CUP LIGHT BROWN SUGAR, PACKED
-    PINCH SALT
- 2 CUPS FINE-CHOPPED WALNUTS
- 2 TEASPOONS PURE VANILLA EXTRACT
- 2½ CUPS UNBLEACHED ALL-PURPOSE FLOUR

Beat the butter and walnut oil together in a large bowl with an electric mixer. Add the sugars and beat well. Add the salt, walnuts, and vanilla extract and mix well. Stir in the flour in three batches, combining well.

Using wax paper to help you, divide the dough into four portions, and roll each into a log about 1 inch in diameter. Refrigerate until very firm, about 4 hours or overnight, rolling the logs two or three times to keep them rounded.

When ready to bake the cookies, preheat the oven to 350° F. Line two or three baking sheets with parchment paper.

Slice the dough about ¼ inch thick. Place the dough rounds on the prepared sheets about an inch apart. Bake the cookies 8 to 10 minutes in the center of the oven, changing the position of the baking sheets about halfway through. The cookies are done when the bottom edges are slightly brown.

Let the cookies cool a minute or two on the baking sheets, then remove to racks to cool completely.

GLAZE AND GARNISH

- ¾ CUP STRAWBERRY PRESERVES
- 2 TABLESPOONS MOSCATO D'ORO WINE
-    ABOUT ½ PINT STRAWBERRIES
- 3 TABLESPOONS CHOPPED FRESH MINT LEAVES

Combine the preserves with the wine and press the mixture through a sieve. Clean and hull the strawberries and slice them about ¼-inch thick.

Brush each cookie lightly with the glaze, place a strawberry slice on top, and sprinkle lightly with the chopped mint. Place the cookies on a platter and serve within a few hours.

SUMMER: SPECTACULAR FIREWORKS

SUMMER

AND A FESTIVE FAMILY FEELING

during the day, the Mondavi family is inclined to eat lighter foods and dishes at this time of year, like others who live with very warm summers. Whether making a menu for entertaining or a family dinner, they look for dishes that highlight the season, and that are simple for everyday cooking. In the markets and their

gardens they find just-harvested peas, strawberries, cherries, and the first peaches in early summer. Midsummer brings vine-ripe tomatoes, tender sweet corn, summer squash with their

tasty blossoms, raspberries, blackberries, and blueberries, more peaches, apricots, and nectarines. Late summer offers eggplant, sweet and hot peppers, summer apples, plums, and figs. Swordfish, tuna, and halibut are most abundant and tasty during the summer.

Dinner is often alfresco, the better to enjoy the cool western evening breezes that come over the hills and make the vines float like flags. Sometimes the meal is a very simple one of pizza with tomatoes and basil from the garden, a salad, and a glass of young red wine. Sometimes the charcoal grill is fired for a nice piece of fresh tuna or swordfish with grilled vegetables. No matter how simple the dishes, however, the food is prepared with care and attention. Margrit believes all of our senses are important whenever we cook, as well as whenever we eat.

In the vineyards, vine shoots are trimmed to keep the plants' energy spent on making fruit, and the rows are weeded regularly. As the season progresses, the fruit swells, making it an attractive snack for birds. If a vineyard is situated where the bird population is large and hungry, netting is put over the vines. Usually, Mylar ribbons tied to vine supports are enough to give the birds pause; they present a surreal visual effect when they flutter. At the

"Sight, smell, touch, and sound let us know how the food will taste. Even before you take a bite of tomato, your hands and nose will let you know if it's ripe. At the stove, the sizzle should be noisier for a sauté than for garlic perfuming the oil."

—MARGRIT BIEVER MONDAVI

wineries, vats, casks, crushers, stemmers—all
the equipment and machinery of wine produc-
tion—are cleaned and put in order in preparation for the harvest.

The Vineyard Room kitchen is even busier
than usual, with the summer concerts and
other entertainments. Chefs and caterers seem
unaffected by the heat of ovens, stoves, and
large outdoor barbecue grills. They have
moments to chat with guests and one another,
to enjoy the abundance of the garden when
they step out the back door. Thyme, parsley,
basil, and rosemary are ringed with flowers—
delphiniums, cornflowers, dahlias, zinnias,
and lisianthus. Artichokes have gone to
brilliant purple-blue thistle flowers. Red
geraniums glow in pots at the garden's periph-
ery. The murmur of many people enjoying
their families, friends, and the festivities min-
gles with the aromas of food and wine.

Fourth of July Concert Dinner

Grilled Swordfish
with Tomato Vinaigrette

FUMÉ BLANC AND CHEVRIGNON

Cucumber Salad

Red Potato Salad

Fried Chicken

MERLOT AND CABERNET SAUVIGNON

Peach and Blackberry Crisp

JOHANNISBERG RIESLING

Cheese and Fruit

*O*f all the events the Mondavi family sponsor at the Oakville winery, the Summer Festival concerts draw the largest audiences. The series opens on the weekend closest to the Fourth of July and presents the jazz and popular music of world-renowned and local musicians, such as Herbie Mann and the Rippingtons. The Preservation Hall Jazz Band of New Orleans has opened the series with their lively interpretations of jazz and blues for the more than quarter century the concerts have been held. The concerts are open to the public, and the proceeds are donated to the Napa Valley Symphony. Most of the audience is from the surrounding community, and many people come year after year for the infectious entertainment, spectacular fireworks, lovely outdoor setting, and festive family feeling.

*G*uests may bring picnics or may choose a catered dinner. Tables are set between the vines, furnished with abundant family-style platters of cooked dishes, salads, and baskets of bread, followed by dessert, cheeses, and seasonal fruits. White wines are served with the lighter courses, followed by red wines for the main and cheese courses.

The menus and food are chosen from a repertoire of old and new favorites, and prepared with care and imagination by Annie Roberts, Vineyard Room chef, and André Mercier and his wife, Rosalie, who have worked with the winery on special events for many years. For those who bring picnics, the Mondavis and the Viviani family, of the Sonoma Cheese Factory, host a wine and cheese tasting during intermission.

hroughout dinner and the concert, it is clear that people have taken to heart the Mondavis' welcome: "We are so glad you could be here tonight. Enjoy the beautiful evening, the wonderful music of the Preservation Hall Jazz Band, and celebrate being in this part of America." The waiting staff that has kept the tables well furnished and clean, the grounds staff that has picked every fallen napkin and paper cup join grandmothers with grandsons, young couples in love, fathers with babies on their shoulders in clapping and dancing as the musicians jam. The band falls silent as everyone turns to the vineyards for the fireworks, presided over by local fire companies. As the fireworks begin, Preservation Hall fuses New Orleans with Francis Scott Key in the national anthem. When the oohs and aahs change to applause for the last multicolored rocket, the guests begin to leave, humming, talking, dancing little two-steps, carrying picnic baskets and small sleepy children.

GRILLED SWORDFISH WITH TOMATO VINAIGRETTE

SERVES 8 AS A FIRST COURSE, 4 TO 6 AS A MAIN COURSE

Annie Roberts uses this dish as a light first course for summer entertaining; the sauce is quite versatile, enhancing full-flavored fish such as salmon and tuna, whether they are grilled, sautéed, poached, or baked. If you can't find the Napa Valley mustard-flavored oil, use olive oil instead, and add ½ teaspoon dry mustard to the food processor with the other ingredients.

TOMATO VINAIGRETTE

- 2 RIPE MEDIUM-SIZE TOMATOES
- ½ CUP NAPA VALLEY MUSTARD-FLAVORED OIL OR OLIVE OIL
- 1½ TEASPOONS FENNEL SEEDS
- 2 TABLESPOONS LEMON JUICE
- 1 TABLESPOON WARM WATER
- SALT AND FRESH-GROUND PEPPER

Core and seed the tomatoes. Quarter them and place in a nonreactive saucepan. Add the oil and fennel seeds and cook over medium heat for about 15 minutes. Remove the pan from the heat and cool to room temperature.

Add the lemon juice and water, and season well with salt and pepper. Place the mixture in a food processor and puree. Strain the vinaigrette, if desired, and chill until ready to serve.

FISH

- 2 POUNDS SWORDFISH OR TUNA STEAK, ABOUT 1 INCH THICK, OR SALMON FILLETS
- ABOUT 2 TABLESPOONS OLIVE OIL
- SALT AND FRESH-GROUND PEPPER

About 30 minutes before you are ready to serve, prepare a medium-hot fire in a grill. Be sure the grill is very clean, as fish sticks easily.

Brush the swordfish all over with the olive oil and season with salt and pepper. When you are ready to grill, rub or brush the grill lightly with oil. Grill the fish about 3 minutes on the first side, repositioning it to make grill marks if you like. Turn and grill 1 to 2 minutes longer, making sure the center stays slightly rare.

Portion the fish and serve it on a warm platter. Pass the vinaigrette.

FRIED CHICKEN

Along with something from the grill, fried chicken practically means outdoor summer dinner. The chicken may be cooked a day ahead, cooled to room temperature, then refrigerated. You can reheat it in a 400° F oven for about 15 minutes, or serve it at cool room temperature, which many people prefer.

2 CHICKENS, 3 TO 3½ POUNDS EACH

4 CUPS BUTTERMILK

1 CUP MILK

1 TEASPOON SALT

¼ TEASPOON TABASCO

2 CUPS UNBLEACHED ALL-PURPOSE FLOUR

2 CUPS FINE DRY BREAD CRUMBS

ABOUT 4 CUPS VEGETABLE OR PEANUT OIL, OR VEGETABLE SHORTENING FOR FRYING

Rinse the chickens well. Cut them into serving pieces and pat dry. Mix the buttermilk, milk, salt, and Tabasco together in a large bowl. Add the chicken pieces and let stand in the refrigerator for at least 2 and up to 8 hours, turning them occasionally.

About an hour before you're ready to cook the chicken, drain the chicken on a rack. Mix the flour and bread crumbs together. Roll the chicken pieces in the mixture, coating each piece very well. Place the pieces on a tray lined with wax paper and refrigerate for 30 minutes to an hour.

Add oil to a depth of ½ inch to each of two heavy frying pans. Heat the oil over medium-high heat until it is hot but not smoking, about 360° F. Add the chicken pieces to the pans, thighs and drumsticks first, then wings and breasts.

Cook until the chicken is golden brown all over, about 10 minutes. Reduce the heat and continue cooking, turning frequently, until the chicken is done, another 10 minutes for breasts and wings, 20 minutes for thighs and drumsticks. Drain the chicken on paper towels and serve hot or at room temperature.

RED POTATO SALAD

This is another dish Annie enjoys serving at summer parties for friends. It is simple in the kitchen, and benefits by being made a few hours ahead, so the flavors can come together.

6 OUNCES PANCETTA, CUT IN ¼-INCH DICE

5 POUNDS SMALL RED POTATOES

⅓ CUP CHAMPAGNE VINEGAR OR WHITE WINE VINEGAR

2 TABLESPOONS DIJON MUSTARD

⅔ CUP OLIVE OIL

4 TO 6 SHALLOTS, DICED FINE

SALT AND FRESH-GROUND PEPPER

¼ CUP CHOPPED FRESH ITALIAN PARSLEY

Cook the pancetta in a small sauté pan over low heat until it is crisp and the fat is rendered. Remove the pancetta to paper towels to drain and discard the fat.

Scrub the potatoes and quarter them. Cook the potatoes in a saucepan of lightly salted boiling water until they are just done, about 10 minutes.

Meanwhile, combine the vinegar and mustard in a bowl. Whisk in the oil to make an emulsion. Whisk in the shallots and season lightly with salt and pepper.

While the potatoes are still warm, toss them with the dressing. Toss in the pancetta and parsley. Season to taste with salt and pepper and adjust the vinegar or olive oil, if desired. Serve warm or at room temperature.

CUCUMBER SALAD

To keep the refreshing crunchiness of the cucumbers, dress the salad 15 or 20 minutes before serving. If you don't have English or Japanese seedless cucumbers, scrape the seeds from other cucumbers with a teaspoon after you have cut them in half.

2 LARGE CUCUMBERS, PREFERABLY ENGLISH OR JAPANESE

4 GREEN ONIONS

3 TO 4 TABLESPOONS RICE VINEGAR

1 TEASPOON SALT

Peel the cucumbers and halve them lengthwise; seed them if necessary, then slice them about ¼ inch thick. Trim the green onions, leaving about 4 inches of green. Slice the onions very thin.

Toss the cucumbers and onions together in a serving bowl. About 15 minutes before serving, sprinkle them with the vinegar and season with salt. Chill; adjust the seasoning just before serving.

PEACH AND BLACKBERRY CRISP

SERVES 6 TO 8

Peaches have a long season in California, from April through September, but most think of them as a high summer fruit. Gary Jenanyan, executive chef of the Great Chefs at the Robert Mondavi Winery Program, has devised this summery dessert to appeal to all ages. A cool glass of dessert wine, such as Moscato d'Oro, sets it off perfectly, and so does ice cream, such as the Lemon Ice Cream on page 218.

FILLING

- **4 LARGE RIPE PEACHES, PREFERABLY FREESTONE, ABOUT 1 ¾ POUNDS**
- **2 CUPS BLACKBERRIES**
- **3 TABLESPOONS UNBLEACHED ALL-PURPOSE FLOUR**
- **2 TABLESPOONS SUGAR**

Preheat the oven to 375° F.

Peel the peaches and slice them about ½ inch thick. Toss them with the berries in a bowl. Sprinkle with the flour and sugar, toss lightly, and place the fruit in a baking dish or deep pie dish.

TOPPING

- **½ CUP FINELY CHOPPED TOASTED ALMONDS OR WALNUTS**
- **1 CUP UNBLEACHED ALL-PURPOSE FLOUR**
- **½ CUP LIGHT BROWN SUGAR, PACKED**
- **1 TABLESPOON GRANULATED SUGAR**
- **¼ TEASPOON GROUND CINNAMON**
- **6 TABLESPOONS UNSALTED BUTTER, AT ROOM TEMPERATURE**

Combine the nuts, flour, sugars, and cinnamon in a large bowl and blend well. Blend in the butter with your fingertips or with a wooden spoon until crumbly.

TO FINISH THE CRISP

Distribute the topping evenly on top of the fruit. Bake for about 35 minutes, or until the crisp has browned nicely, and the juices from the fruit are bubbling. Remove the crisp from the oven and cool for at least 20 minutes, or up to several hours, before serving.

Lunch from the Farmers' Market

Pastina in Brodo

Ratatouille

Corn on the Cob

Garden Lettuce with

Margrit's Balsamic Vinaigrette

Parmesan Cheese

FUMÉ BLANC AND PINOT NOIR

Blueberry Pie

Growing up in the Canton Ticino of Switzerland gave Margrit an abiding appreciation of the fruits of the earth. Her family grew everything they consumed on their estate—garden vegetables and herbs, apples, pears, and grapes (and kept poultry). Her mother, poised and elegant, took the responsibility of butchering chickens and bartering foodstuffs during the Second World War. For Margrit's father, the family dinner was the most important event of the day; he took great interest in what the children were doing and thinking, as well as in the food and wine of the meal.

With this background, Margrit relishes the good local produce and cheeses, and the opportunity to do much of her marketing at farmers' markets. Though she keeps a small kitchen garden for tomatoes, chili peppers, lettuces, basil, Italian parsley, and other herbs, she enjoys meeting friends and the growers who've become friends at the two markets she goes to weekly.

Lunch at home on workdays is usually light, but with a variety of courses and tastes to make it a refreshing break. Robert and Margrit are early risers; they swim exercise laps in the pool before breakfast, and often leave to arrive at the winery at eight or eight-thirty.

Before Margrit leaves, she does such preparations as mixing pie dough, rolling it out, and freezing it.

On this day, the Mondavis serve a European-style lunch, the main meal of the day. Robert sets out the wineglasses for Fumé Blanc and Pinot Noir while Margrit draws a menu, illustrating the vibrant vegetables in the ratatouille. The natural warmth with which they entertain their guests, the zest and sense of fun with which they make a simple lunch an occasion, are characteristic. As Robert says, "Living well is something we can all do every day."

Pastina in Brodo

Pastina in brodo is one of Margrit's favorite first courses; it is light, and adaptable to many menus. In the method she uses for making broth in the following recipe, which Margrit has used for many years, there are two bonuses: The broth is done overnight, and there is a poached chicken for another dish. The broth is light, but flavorful. When Margrit has a leek, she adds it to the broth; if she doesn't have a bell pepper, she adds a small dried red chili for a hint of capsicum flavor.

4 CUPS CHICKEN BROTH (RECIPE FOLLOWS)
2 OUNCES CAPELLINI OR ANGEL HAIR PASTA
ZEST FROM ½ LEMON, CUT IN LONG, THIN STRIPS
CHOPPED FRESH ITALIAN PARSLEY, FOR GARNISH

Be sure the broth is seasoned to your liking. Add it to a pot and bring it to a gentle boil. Break the dry pasta strands in five or six pieces and add them to the broth. Cook until the pasta is al dente.

Place the lemon zest in four soup plates or bowls. Divide the broth and pasta among the bowls. Garnish with Italian parsley and serve hot.

CHICKEN BROTH

1 WHOLE CHICKEN, ABOUT 3 POUNDS

3 CELERY STALKS, CUT IN THIRDS

2 CARROTS, PEELED AND CUT IN THIRDS

1 ONION, QUARTERED

½ GREEN BELL PEPPER, SEEDED

3 GARLIC CLOVES, PEELED

SALT

Rinse the chicken well. Place it, breast up, along with the vegetables and garlic, in a stockpot. Cover with cold water and bring to a boil over high heat. As the water comes to a boil, the chicken will release protein foam. Watch carefully, and skim off the foam. Boil the liquid for 5 minutes, then turn off the heat and skim off any remaining foam. Cover with a tight-fitting lid and let the chicken stand in the broth overnight, or at least 8 hours at cool room temperature.

The next morning, check the thigh of the chicken to see if the meat is cooked to the bone. If it is not, bring the broth to a boil and simmer until the thighs are cooked. Remove the chicken to a platter and reserve for another use.

Strain the broth into a clean pan. Taste the broth and reduce it by about one fourth to concentrate the flavor. Salt to taste. If you are using the broth immediately, degrease it with a skimmer or a spoon. If you will be using the broth later, cool it to room temperature, then refrigerate to facilitate degreasing.

RATATOUILLE

Margrit says, "In cooking, taste is the most fundamental thing; every ingredient changes every day. What I taste for is the balance of sour and sweet, then bitter and salt. When I use eggplant, I smell them after trimming the ends, to see if they are bitter. Some techniques I follow are ones I learned from my mother. She never covered zucchini while they were cooking; there may or may not be a reason for this, but I still don't cover them."

1 RED ONION, ABOUT 8 OUNCES, DICED

1 OR 2 GARLIC CLOVES, MINCED

2 TABLESPOONS EXTRA-VIRGIN OLIVE OIL

1 GREEN BELL PEPPER, ABOUT 8 OUNCES, DICED

1 EGGPLANT, ABOUT 1 POUND, TRIMMED AND DICED

2   SMALL YELLOW CROOKNECK SQUASH, ABOUT 4 OUNCES EACH, DICED

2   SMALL ZUCCHINI, ABOUT 4 OUNCES EACH, DICED

2   POUNDS RIPE TOMATOES, DICED

3   OR 4 FRESH ITALIAN PARSLEY SPRIGS, LEAVES CHOPPED

OPTIONAL: 1 SMALL DRIED HOT PEPPER

2   OR 3 LARGE FRESH BASIL SPRIGS, 1 LEFT WHOLE, REMAINDER OF LEAVES CHOPPED

SALT AND FRESH-GROUND PEPPER

Soften the onion and garlic in the oil in a large sauté pan over medium heat. Add the green pepper, eggplant, yellow squash, and zucchini. Season lightly with salt and pepper and sauté the vegetables until softened, 5 to 10 minutes, stirring occasionally.

Add the tomatoes, parsley, and dried hot pepper if you are using it. Cook, uncovered, until the vegetables are just firm-tender, 15 to 20 minutes. Add the chopped basil during the last few minutes of cooking. Adjust the seasoning and serve hot, garnished with the basil sprigs.

GARDEN LETTUCE
WITH MARGRIT'S BALSAMIC VINAIGRETTE   SERVES 4

Margrit and several friends and neighbors have begun to make balsamic vinegar in Napa Valley. They hope that the centuries-old tradition of balsamic vinegar-making in Modena, Italy, can take root in another region where wine grapes are grown. They consulted the subject's most noted Italian authority for information on the cooking of the grape must, the several kinds of wooden barrels necessary to impart complex flavors to the vinegar, and the schedules of barrel transfers and blending. The group's effort has been rewarded by a balsamic vinegar that is rich, with definite yet subtle flavors and texture. Some bitter greens, such as radicchio, endive, or escarole, in the salad are particularly interesting with the vinegar.

1 QUART MIXED SALAD GREENS, WASHED AND DRIED

1 TABLESPOON EXTRA-VIRGIN OLIVE OIL

ABOUT 1 TEASPOON BALSAMIC VINEGAR

SALT AND FRESH-GROUND PEPPER

Toss the greens with the olive oil. Sprinkle the vinegar over, add a pinch of salt and a grinding or two of pepper and toss again. Adjust the seasoning with a few drops of vinegar, salt, or pepper if necessary. Serve immediately.

Blueberry Pie

In summer, everyone enjoys the seasonal treat of Sonoma County blueberries, available from the local farmers' markets, to fill the prebaked crust. The pie is practically pure fruit, heaven for blueberry lovers. You will need half of the pastry dough for this pie; freeze the other portion of dough for another pie.

PASTRY DOUGH (RECIPE FOLLOWS)

2 PINTS BLUEBERRIES

1 TO 2 TABLESPOONS SUGAR

ABOUT 1 TEASPOON LEMON JUICE

OPTIONAL: ABOUT 1 CUP WHIPPING CREAM

Divide the dough in half and roll one portion to fit a 9-inch pie plate; reserve the other portion for another use. Place the pie shell in the freezer while you prepare the blueberries. Preheat the oven to 400° F.

Rinse and sort through the blueberries, reserving about one third of the plumpest and best-looking for the topping. Place the remaining berries in a nonreactive saucepan and cook them just until the berries burst, about 5 minutes. Taste them and sprinkle with a little sugar and lemon juice to heighten their flavor. Cool the berries to room temperature.

While you are letting the berries cool, prebake the pie crust. Line the pie dough with aluminum foil and fill it with beans or pie weights. Bake for 10 minutes. Remove the foil and weights and reduce the heat to 375° F. Bake the crust until it is a rich golden brown, 10 to 15 minutes. Remove to a rack to cool.

When the filling and crust are at room temperature, spoon the cooked berries into the crust, leaving runny juices in the pan. Reduce the juices to the consistency of thin jam and spoon over the berries. Cover the pie with the fresh blueberries. Let the pie stand a few minutes before cutting and serving. If you like, whip some cream lightly and garnish each serving with a dollop of whipped cream.

PASTRY DOUGH

Margrit makes most of her pies and tarts with a dough that she has found tasty and reliable for years, a kind of pâte brisée. It has the advantage that it needs only a short rest in the freezer before baking to a short, crisp crust. If you need only one portion of dough, freeze the other. You can roll it and freeze it in a pie plate or tart shell; in that case, bake it according to recipe instructions without defrosting. If you freeze it unrolled, defrost it in the refrigerator overnight before rolling.

2 CUPS UNBLEACHED ALL-PURPOSE FLOUR

1 CUP (8 OUNCES) CHILLED UNSALTED BUTTER, QUARTERED LENGTHWISE AND CUT INTO PIECES

1 TEASPOON SALT

1 LARGE EGG, LIGHTLY BEATEN

2 TABLESPOONS MILK

Combine all the ingredients in a food processor and process until the dough gathers and just begins to turn over the top, about a minute. Remove the dough to a work surface and divide it into two portions. Press each portion into a round about ½ inch thick. Place each round between two sheets of plastic wrap or wax paper and roll to fit two 9-inch pie plates or tart pans; fit the dough into the pie plates or tart pans and crimp the edges. Or, wrap the dough well, and freeze for up to a month, defrosting in the refrigerator overnight before rolling.

After rolling and fitting, place the dough in the freezer for 15 to 30 minutes before prebaking or filling.

Opus One Picnic

Whole Poached Salmon
with Wasabi Mayonnaise

Fennel and Cucumber Salad

Baskets of Grilled Quail

OPUS ONE AND MOUTON CADET

Fig, Plum, or Nectarine Tarts

French and American Cheeses and Breads

The Opus One Winery picnic for employees was part of the 1994 Labor Day Weekend celebration to commemorate many milestones at the winery. As at any company picnic, employees and their families were treated to food, entertainment, games, and a good time outside of the usual protocols of business. Opus One makes a very special wine, and 1994 was the release of the 1991 vintage, the first made in the winery's own facility. The food, wine, and fun at the picnic were special as well. Opus One wine is the creation of Baron Philippe de Rothschild and Robert Mondavi, crafted to bring together the finest of Bordeaux and Napa Valley winemaking techniques and conditions. This year also marked the twenty-fifth anniversary of the first Opus One vintage, 1979, and the third anniversary of the winery's visually striking, curved main building and entrance courtyard.

To emphasize the fruitful relationship of Franco-American food and wine, the winery chose Michel Cornu to cater the picnic. Michel and his wife, Annelise, are Parisians who moved to the Napa Valley some

fifteen years ago, where they are raising their children, along with sheep, geese, ducks, and chickens, and tending various orchards and gardens in a country-suburban setting. Michel's picnic fare was seasonal, bountiful, and a blend of the rustic and elegant. To please children and adults, he made three kinds of "French hot dogs"—pork, veal, and seafood—as well as grilled vegetables, fruit salad, and chocolate cake.

The picnic was held in an old oak grove between the vineyards and the Napa River, a setting that provided welcome shade on the hot afternoon. The grove echoed with youngsters' voices playing tag and laughing at the clowns, then more softly as everyone found places at tables set with sunflowers and Queen Anne's lace. Tarts, cheeses, fruit salad, and cake replaced the main courses and salads. Re-energized, the children once again roamed the grove while the adults settled into talk, cooling evening shadows, and country-western tunes.

Whole Salmon with Wasabi Mayonnaise

The salmon is not only tasty and impressive looking, but Michel Cornu's method of preparing it is simple. If you don't have sturdy kitchen shears, ask your fishmonger to remove the center bone from the tail end of the cavity to the head. It is best to poach the salmon the evening before it is to be served and decorate it the next morning. If the fish is kept well chilled after removing it from the poaching liquid, it can be poached two days ahead and decorated the day it is served. You will need a fish poacher or roasting pan large enough to hold the fish without curling. If you use a roasting pan, you will need at least double the amount of court bouillon.

SALMON AND GARNISH

- 4 QUARTS WATER
- 1 BOTTLE (750 ML) DRY WHITE WINE
- 2 LEMONS, SLICED
- 8 TO 10 FRESH ITALIAN PARSLEY SPRIGS
- 2 BAY LEAVES
- 1 TABLESPOON PLUS 1 TEASPOON SALT
- 1 WHOLE SALMON, 7 TO 8 POUNDS
- 6 TO 8 FRESH BASIL SPRIGS
- 1 SEEDLESS CUCUMBER, ENGLISH OR JAPANESE
- 1 PACKAGE ASPIC MIX
- 1 TABLESPOON DRY VERMOUTH
- 1 TABLESPOON PERNOD OR RICARD

GARNISH: SEAWEED AND/OR EDIBLE LEAVES OR FLOWERS

Bring the water, wine, lemons, parsley, bay leaves, and salt to a simmer. Cook, uncovered, for 20 minutes, then strain. Meanwhile, rinse the salmon and slit the cavity with a sharp knife from tail end to head. Place the fish so you can see and feel the center bone. Cut it at head and tail with heavy kitchen shears. With a small sharp knife, work the bone free from the flesh. Using needle-nosed pliers, remove the small, flexible lateral bones.

Fill the cavity with the basil sprigs and wrap the salmon well in rinsed cheesecloth. Beginning at the head, tie kitchen twine around the salmon. Wrap the twine around the fish tightly on a diagonal, and finish with a knot at the tail end, taking care that the tail is not curled. Place the salmon in a fish poacher or roasting pan and cover with court bouillon by about an inch.

Bring the liquid to a simmer over medium-high heat. Reduce the heat to keep the liquid barely bubbling for 45 minutes. Turn the heat off and let the fish cool in the poacher to room temperature. Refrigerate the fish overnight.

When ready to decorate the salmon, remove the cheesecloth. Remove the skin from the fish, except for the head and tail, working carefully from the cavity to the back on each side. Place the salmon on a serving platter.

Divide the aspic mix in half and follow the package directions for making the aspic, adjusting the proportion of liquid. Add the vermouth and Pernod to the hot liquid. Refrigerate the aspic until it just begins to gel.

Meanwhile, peel the cucumber and slice it very thin, about 1/16 inch. Dip the cucumber slices in the aspic, one at a time, and, beginning at the tail, overlap them slightly to make a decorative pattern. Surround the salmon with seaweed and/or edible leaves and flowers.

WASABI MAYONNAISE

2 LARGE EGG YOLKS

ABOUT 1 TABLESPOON LEMON JUICE

1 1/2 CUPS OLIVE OIL

2 TEASPOONS WASABI POWDER, OR TO TASTE

1/2 TEASPOON MUSTARD POWDER

1 TABLESPOON WARM WATER

SALT AND FRESH-GROUND PEPPER

To make the mayonnaise by hand: Whisk the egg yolks with about 1 tablespoon of lemon juice. Add the olive oil, a few drops at a time, then in a thin stream, whisking continually until the mayonnaise emulsifies. Mix the wasabi and mustard powders with the warm water, then whisk the mixture into the mayonnaise. Adjust the seasoning with lemon juice, salt, and pepper.

To make the mayonnaise in a food processor: Pulse the egg yolks with about 1 table-spoon of lemon juice. Add the oil in a thin stream with the motor running until the mayonnaise emulsifies, then transfer the mayonnaise to a bowl. Mix the wasabi and mustard and add to the mayonnaise as above. Adjust the seasoning.

Cover the mayonnaise and keep refrigerated until ready to serve.

Fennel and Cucumber Salad

This salad is refreshing served with the salmon, as it provides a naturally sweet-tart contrast to the salmon's slightly rich and spicy flavor. If you don't have tarragon or lemon vinegar, use white wine vinegar and add about a teaspoon of grated lemon zest.

1 ½   POUNDS FENNEL

2   SEEDLESS CUCUMBERS, ENGLISH OR JAPANESE

2   TABLESPOONS TARRAGON OR LEMON VINEGAR

1   TABLESPOON CHOPPED FRESH TARRAGON LEAVES

1   TEASPOON SALT

¼   CUP HAZELNUT OIL

ABOUT ½ TEASPOON FRESH-GROUND WHITE PEPPER

6   OUNCES BEAN SPROUTS

Trim the fennel of stems and tough outer leaves. Poach it in simmering water to cover for 5 minutes. Drain and refresh under cold water, then slice the fennel lengthwise about ⅛ inch thick. Cut the slices into matchsticks and place in a serving dish.

Peel the cucumbers, halve them lengthwise, and slice about ⅛ inch thick. Add to the dish with the fennel.

Make a vinaigrette by combining the vinegar, tarragon, and salt in a bowl. Whisk the oil into the vinegar to make an emulsion, then season with the white pepper. Toss half the vinaigrette with the fennel and cucumbers and refrigerate.

Twenty or 30 minutes before you're ready to serve, add the bean sprouts to the fennel and cucumber. Toss with the remaining vinaigrette and adjust the seasoning. Keep cool until ready to serve.

GRILLED QUAIL

Boneless quail are only partially boned; the thigh, drumstick, and wing bones are left in. The quail may be grilled about 30 minutes ahead to serve at room temperature; they should rest for 5 minutes so they are juicy and guests don't burn their fingers. The recipe is easily halved if you are serving a smaller number of people.

Mirin is a sweet Japanese rice wine. It is available in many supermarkets, but dry sherry may be substituted.

24	BONELESS FRESH QUAIL
1	CUP DRY WHITE WINE
½	CUP WALNUT OIL
⅓	CUP TERIYAKI SAUCE
¼	CUP MIRIN
8	TO 10 SPRIGS FRESH LEMON THYME OR REGULAR THYME
2	LARGE SHALLOTS, ABOUT 2 OUNCES
	SALT AND FRESH-GROUND PEPPER

Rinse the quail and pat them dry. Place them in a bowl, or in a large plastic bag that can be completely sealed. Mix the wine, walnut oil, teriyaki sauce, and mirin in a bowl. Bruise the thyme sprigs and add them to the marinade. Peel and slice the shallots and add them to the marinade. Season it lightly with salt and pepper. Pour the marinade over the quail and mix well. Cover or seal and marinate in the refrigerator for 24 hours, turning the quail two or three times.

About an hour before you're ready to grill the quail, remove them from the refrigerator and let stand. Meanwhile, prepare a medium-hot grill.

When the coals are medium hot, place the quail on the grill and grill for about 6 minutes on each side, turning them frequently. The quail should be cooked rare to medium-rare and nicely colored. Remove to a basket lined with grape leaves, or a serving platter. Serve hot or at room temperature.

Michel made several of these for the picnic. He describes them as "simple, grandmother-style tarts." They are the essence of the fruit, enriched a bit by the crust, just a sprinkling of sugar, and a few dots of butter. You can make a single tart by halving the recipe if you wish. For the best results, use perfectly ripe fruit. If you use firm-ripe fruit, the tarts will not have the lovely fruit juices. Since the tarts are juicy, they should be served a few hours after baking.

PASTRY DOUGH (PAGE 193)

2 POUNDS FIGS OR 2½ POUNDS FREESTONE PLUMS OR NECTARINES

3 TABLESPOONS SUGAR

2 TABLESPOONS UNSALTED BUTTER, CUT IN SMALL BITS

Roll the portions of dough to fit two 9-inch tart pans with removable bottoms. Cover and set in the freezer for at least 15 minutes. Preheat the oven to 400° F.

After the dough has rested, line it with foil and fill with beans or pie weights. Bake for 15 minutes. Remove the foil and weights, reduce the oven temperature to 375° F, and bake for 5 minutes, until the crusts are set and pale golden. Remove the tart pans to a rack while you prepare the fruit.

Wash the figs, pat dry, halve them lengthwise, and remove any tough stems. Or, wash the plums or nectarines, halve them lengthwise, and remove the stones.

Arrange the fruit decoratively, cut sides up, in the tart shells. Sprinkle with a little sugar and dot with the butter. Bake the tarts for 20 to 30 minutes, until the fruit is tender and juicy and the crust golden brown. Cool to room temperature on a rack before cutting.

SUMMER RECIPES

BRUSCHETTA

This version of the Italian snack/appetizer is one that Margrit and Annie find welcome whenever flavorful fresh tomatoes are in season. The herbs here go well with Fumé Blanc, but try the bruschetta with any of your favorite summer or fall appetizer wines. The tomato-herb mixture is best made a few hours ahead to allow the flavors time to marry.

1 POUND ITALIAN OR FRENCH COUNTRY-STYLE
  BREAD
ABOUT ⅓ CUP EXTRA-VIRGIN OLIVE OIL
1 POUND RIPE PLUM OR OTHER TOMATOES
1 OR 2 GARLIC CLOVES, MINCED
6 TO 8 FRESH BASIL LEAVES, CHOPPED
6 TO 8 FRESH ITALIAN PARSLEY SPRIGS, LEAVES
  CHOPPED
¼ CUP CHOPPED GREEN ONION OR SHALLOT
¼ CUP FINE-DICED GREEN BELL PEPPER
SPLASH OF WHITE OR RED WINE VINEGAR
½ TEASPOON SALT

Preheat the oven to 350° F.

Slice the bread about ½ inch thick and place on baking sheets. Brush each slice lightly with olive oil. Bake until the bread is golden and crisp on top, about 15 minutes.

Peel and seed the tomatoes if desired, then dice and place in a bowl. Add the remaining ingredients including the remaining olive oil. Let the mixture stand for at least an hour at cool room temperature.

When ready to serve, adjust the seasoning. To serve, spoon some tomato mixture on each bread slice, pressing the tomatoes and their juices lightly into the toasted bread. Serve immediately.

MARGRIT'S SUMMER PASTA

Margrit says, "All kinds of wine go with this dish—Fumé Blanc, Pinot Noir, Merlot, or a young Cabernet Sauvignon. I prefer feta with pasta in the summer because it tastes lighter to me than Parmesan."

This is a very Italian summer pasta, with the flavor of ripe tomatoes, a few herb leaves and olives to lend liveliness, and the sauce just coating the pasta. The sauce can be made while the pasta is cooking.

1 TABLESPOON OLIVE OIL
3 GARLIC CLOVES, MINCED
5 OR 6 GREEN ONIONS, SLICED THIN WITH 2 INCHES
  OF GREEN
2 POUNDS RIPE TOMATOES OR CHERRY TOMATOES
SALT AND FRESH-GROUND PEPPER
1 POUND PENNE OR BOW-TIE PASTA
3 LARGE FRESH BASIL SPRIGS, LEAVES SHREDDED
3 ITALIAN PARSLEY SPRIGS, LEAVES CHOPPED FINE
ABOUT 15 KALAMATA OLIVES, PITTED AND CHOPPED
  COARSE
1 CUP CRUMBLED FETA CHEESE, OR ½ CUP FRESHLY
  GRATED ITALIAN PARMESAN CHEESE

Place a large pot of cold water over high heat. Add the olive oil to a large sauté pan over medium heat. Add the garlic and green onions and soften.

Meanwhile, core, seed, and dice the tomatoes or stem and halve the cherry tomatoes. Add the tomatoes to the sauté pan and season with salt and pepper.

When the water boils, add about a tablespoon of salt and stir in the pasta. Cook the sauce over low heat while the pasta cooks. If the tomatoes are watery, increase the heat and reduce the sauce a bit.

When the pasta is al dente, drain it and add to the sauce. Toss together with the basil, parsley, and olives. Garnish with feta or Parmesan cheese and serve.

QUICK FRESH TOMATO PIZZA

SERVES 4 TO 8

Because she uses rapid-rise yeast, Margrit can make this pizza after she comes home from work. The pizza is hearty enough for a main course, or may be served as an appetizer. Serve it with an uncomplicated, young red wine.

DOUGH

- **1 PACKAGE RAPID-RISE YEAST**
- **1 CUP WARM (100 TO 105° F) WATER**
- **¼ CUP OLIVE OIL**
- **ABOUT 3 CUPS UNBLEACHED ALL-PURPOSE FLOUR**
- **¼ CUP CORNMEAL**
- **1 TEASPOON SALT**

Dissolve the yeast in the water in a large bowl. When the yeast is foamy, stir in the oil, 3 cups flour, cornmeal, and salt. Knead the dough briefly; if it is sticky, add more flour, ¼ cup at a time. Knead the dough until it is smooth, about 5 minutes. Place the dough in a bowl and cover with plastic wrap. Let the dough rise in a warm place while you make the topping.

TOPPING AND ASSEMBLY

- **4 TO 6 RIPE TOMATOES, PREFERABLY ROMA OR OTHER ITALIAN PLUM TYPE**
- **3 OR 4 FRESH BASIL SPRIGS**
- **8 OUNCES FRESH MOZZARELLA CHEESE**
- **4 OUNCES MONTEREY JACK CHEESE**
- **2 OUNCES ITALIAN PARMESAN CHEESE**
- **OPTIONAL: ¼ POUND PROSCIUTTO OR BLACK FOREST HAM**
- **CORNMEAL FOR SPRINKLING**
- **2 TABLESPOONS OLIVE OIL**
- **SALT AND FRESH-GROUND PEPPER**

Slice the tomatoes about ¼ inch thick. Remove the basil leaves and shred them. Grate the cheeses. If you are using prosciutto or ham, slice it in strips about ⅛ inch wide.

When the dough has almost doubled in bulk, about 30 minutes, divide it into four portions. Form each portion into a disk, cover with plastic wrap, and let rest for 5 or 10 minutes. Meanwhile, preheat the oven to 500° F. Place baking sheets each large enough to hold two 8-inch pizzas in the oven.

Stretch and pat the dough into 8-inch circles with slightly thicker rims. When the baking sheets are hot, sprinkle them with cornmeal. Place the pizza dough on the sheets and bake for 5 minutes.

Remove the pizzas from the oven and brush them with the olive oil. Layer the pizzas with the cheeses, tomatoes, and prosciutto or ham, if desired. Salt and pepper lightly. Bake until the crusts are golden brown and the cheese is just melted and bubbling, about 7 minutes. Garnish with the basil shreds and serve hot.

FUSILLI WITH VINEGAR-MARINATED ZUCCHINI

Marcella Hazan's recipe exemplifies why she is a master of Italian cooking and of communicating the essence of a dish in recipe form. The dish is as clear, direct, and satisfying to eat as the recipe is to read and follow. Marcella prepared the dish, from her book *Marcella's Italian Kitchen,* for the Great Chefs at the Robert Mondavi Winery Program. Her Lemon Ice Cream, from the same book, can be found here on page 218. For making the dish ahead, Marcella writes: "The zucchini may be prepared two or three days ahead of time. Refrigerate them with their marinade in a covered container. Turn them occasionally. Make sure to bring them back to room temperature before you cook the pasta."

3 POUNDS FRESH, GLOSSY ZUCCHINI, ABOUT 6 INCHES LONG

SALT

VEGETABLE OIL FOR FRYING

3 TABLESPOONS RED WINE VINEGAR

1 GARLIC CLOVE, MINCED

10 TO 15 MINT LEAVES, TORN BY HAND INTO SMALL BITS

⅓ CUP EXTRA-VIRGIN OLIVE OIL

BLACK PEPPER IN A GRINDER

1 POUND FUSILLI

Scrub the zucchini well to remove any grit. Trim the ends and cut the zucchini into sticks about 2 inches long and ¼ inch thick.

Set a large colander over a bowl or basin and place the zucchini in the colander. Sprinkle them with 2 tablespoons salt, turn them two or three times, and allow them to sit for at least 45 minutes to drain them of as much liquid as possible.

If you have a deep-fat fryer, pour enough vegetable oil in to rise 4 inches up the side of the pan. If you are using a frying pan, the oil should be 1½ inches deep, if possible. Turn on the heat to medium high.

When you are ready to begin frying, remove the zucchini sticks from the colander and blot them thoroughly dry in kitchen towels. As soon as the oil is hot, about 360° F, drop as many zucchini sticks into the pan as will fit without crowding.

Watch carefully; the moment the zucchini become light brown, about 2 minutes, transfer them with a strainer directly to the bowl where you will later toss the pasta.

When you have finished frying the zucchini sticks and placed them all in the bowl, pour the vinegar over them and turn them once or twice. Add the garlic, mint, olive oil, and a few grindings of pepper. Mix well, and adjust the seasonings with salt, pepper, or vinegar.

Cook the pasta in a pot of abundant boiling salted water until it is just tender and firm to the bite. Drain, toss immediately with the zucchini, and serve. No cheese is required or desirable with this dish.

ROASTED RED AND YELLOW PEPPER SOUP WITH BASIL CREAM

Though Sarah Scott created this dish as a cold soup, it is delicious hot or warm as well. It can precede almost any summer main course. Fumé Blanc is a good wine with the vegetable and herb flavors.

- **4 RED BELL PEPPERS, ROASTED, PEELED, SEEDED, AND DEVEINED (PAGE 133)**
- **4 YELLOW BELL PEPPERS, ROASTED, PEELED, SEEDED, AND DEVEINED (PAGE 133)**
- **2 TABLESPOONS OLIVE OIL**
- **2 ONIONS, HALVED LENGTHWISE AND SLICED THIN**
- **8 CUPS CHICKEN BROTH**
- **1 TO 2 TABLESPOONS BALSAMIC VINEGAR**
- **1 TO 2 TABLESPOONS EXTRA-VIRGIN OLIVE OIL**
- **SALT AND FRESH-GROUND PEPPER**
- **1 CUP FRESH BASIL LEAVES**
- **⅓ CUP SOUR CREAM**
- **2 TO 3 TABLESPOONS MILK**

Collect any juices that have collected from the peppers as you work with them. Heat the olive oil in a sauté pan over medium heat. Add the sliced onions and cook for about 5 minutes. Turn the heat to low and add 1 cup of the chicken broth. Cook slowly, uncovered, until the onions are softened, about 15 minutes, stirring occasionally.

Place the red bell peppers, half of the onion mixture, and 3 cups of the chicken broth in a blender or food processor. Puree well, then add about ½ tablespoon each balsamic vinegar and extra-virgin olive oil and a pinch of salt and pepper. Puree again, then taste, adding additional vinegar, oil, salt, or pepper as needed. The soup should be the consistency of whipping cream.

Pour the soup into a storage pitcher, rinse the blender or processor, and repeat the process with the yellow bell peppers and remaining onion. Pour this soup into another storage pitcher and refrigerate the soups at least 4 hours, or overnight.

Taste the soups for seasoning just before serving, and thin with a little chicken broth if necessary.

Blanch the basil leaves in boiling water for 2 seconds. Drain and place in ice water. Drain again and squeeze most liquid from the basil. Place the basil in a blender or food processor with the sour cream and 2 tablespoons milk. Puree until very smooth and the consistency of light cream. Season with salt and pepper and thin with more milk if necessary.

To serve, pour the red and yellow soups simultaneously from both sides into wide soup bowls. Drizzle with the basil cream.

SEARED HALIBUT WITH WHITE BEANS AND WARM VINAIGRETTE

Tuscans are partial to the combination of fish and beans, a combination that finds a very flavorful form in this Annie Roberts dish. It needs only bread and wine to accompany it; Annie is partial to Pinot Noir for this. The beans may be made a day or two ahead and reheated gently to finish the dish.

BEANS

- 1 CUP DRIED SMALL WHITE BEANS
- 1 TABLESPOON OLIVE OIL
- 4 OUNCES PANCETTA OR BACON, SLICED THIN AND CHOPPED COARSE
- 1 LARGE SHALLOT, MINCED
- 2 GARLIC CLOVES, MINCED
- 1 FRESH THYME SPRIG, LEAVES MINCED, OR ½ TEASPOON DRIED THYME
- 1 FRESH ITALIAN PARSLEY SPRIG, LEAVES MINCED
- 4 CUPS CHICKEN BROTH
- SALT AND FRESH GROUND PEPPER
- 1 POUND RIPE TOMATOES, PEELED, SEEDED, AND DICED

Soak the beans overnight in cold water to cover by 2 or 3 inches. Drain and rinse the beans and place them in a large nonreactive saucepan. Or, bring 2 or 3 quarts of water to a boil, add the beans and return to a boil. Cover the pan and remove from the heat. Let the beans stand for an hour, then drain and rinse them, and return them to the pan.

Heat the olive oil in a sauté pan over low heat. Add the pancetta and shallot and cook for 5 minutes. Add the garlic, thyme, and parsley and cook for 10 minutes. Add the mixture to the beans along with the chicken broth. Cook until the beans are just tender and season with salt and pepper. Add the tomatoes when ready to finish the dish.

SALAD AND FISH

- 2 TABLESPOONS RED WINE VINEGAR
- 1 TABLESPOON DIJON MUSTARD
- 1 TEASPOON DICED SHALLOT
- ¼ CUP EXTRA-VIRGIN OLIVE OIL
- SALT AND FRESH-GROUND PEPPER
- 4 HALIBUT FILLETS, ABOUT 4 OUNCES EACH
- 1 TABLESPOON OLIVE OIL
- 1 QUART MIXED SALAD GREENS, CLEANED AND DRIED

Combine the vinegar, mustard, and shallot in a bowl. Whisk in the extra-virgin olive oil to make an emulsion. Season with salt and pepper; transfer to a small nonreactive saucepan, and warm over low heat.

Gently reheat the beans and tomatoes. Toss the salad greens with half the warm vinaigrette and arrange around the edges of a serving platter or plates.

Season the halibut lightly with salt and pepper. Heat a nonstick sauté pan large enough to hold the fish without crowding over high heat. Add the olive oil and the halibut. Cook the fish until the bottom is well browned and the edges are opaque, about 4 minutes. Turn the fish and cook for 1 minute. Remove the fish to a plate.

Spoon the beans over the center of the platter or plates. Place the halibut on the beans. Drizzle with the remaining vinaigrette and serve immediately.

ORIENTAL-STYLE CHICKEN SALAD

This light main course is one of Margrit's favorites for really hot summer days—refreshing yet flavorful, and easy for the cook. Fumé Blanc is the perfect wine with it. The recipe may be doubled.

- **3 CUPS CHICKEN BROTH**
- **1 CUP FUMÉ BLANC OR OTHER DRY WHITE WINE**
- **4 BONELESS, SKINLESS CHICKEN BREAST HALVES**
- **¼ CUP SOY SAUCE**
- **¼ CUP RICE VINEGAR**
- **1 GARLIC CLOVE, MINCED**
- **½ TEASPOON RED PEPPER FLAKES, OR TO TASTE**
- **¼ CUP PEANUT OIL**
- **1 TABLESPOON DARK SESAME OIL**
- **1 SEEDLESS ENGLISH OR JAPANESE CUCUMBER, PEELED AND CUT INTO MATCHSTICKS**
- **3 GREEN ONIONS WITH 4 INCHES OF GREEN, SLICED ON A DIAGONAL**
- **3 OR 4 FRESH CILANTRO SPRIGS, LEAVES CHOPPED**
- **¼ CUP ROASTED PEANUTS, CHOPPED**
- **1 TABLESPOON SESAME SEEDS, LIGHTLY TOASTED IN A SMALL SKILLET**

Combine the chicken broth and wine in a pan large enough to hold the chicken and bring to a simmer. Add the chicken breasts and poach until just cooked through, about 10 minutes. Remove the chicken to a plate to cool. Reserve the broth for another use, if desired.

Meanwhile, make the vinaigrette. Combine the soy sauce, vinegar, garlic, and red pepper flakes in a bowl. Whisk in the peanut and sesame oil to make an emulsion.

When the chicken is cool enough to handle, tear it in shreds and place it on a serving dish. Add the cucumber, green onions, and cilantro. Toss with the vinaigrette. Cover the dish and refrigerate for 30 minutes or so.

Just before serving, toss in the peanuts and sesame seeds.

ROY YAMAGUCHI'S SEARED SWORDFISH WITH LEMONGRASS CRUST AND THAI PEANUT SAUCE

Roy Yamaguchi presented this dish with a Pinot Noir Reserve when he participated in the Great Chefs at the Robert Mondavi Winery Program in 1994. It is typical of Roy's Euro-Asian cooking: The complex flavors of Asian ingredients are combined using European methods, resulting in food that is multilayered with flavor, yet light to eat. Drawing on his experiences in Japan, New York, and California, Roy creates his delicious dishes in Roy's Restaurant in Honolulu.

The peanut sauce may be made a day or two ahead and finished just before cooking the swordfish. You will need only ½ cup of the sauce to use with the fish. The remainder may be used with other Oriental dishes, such as satays.

PEANUT SAUCE

- 2 CUPS CANNED UNSWEETENED COCONUT MILK
- ⅓ CUP PLUS 1 TABLESPOON DARK BROWN SUGAR, PACKED
- 5 TABLESPOONS CREAMY PEANUT BUTTER
- 2½ TABLESPOONS SOY SAUCE
- 2½ TABLESPOONS LEMON JUICE
- 1 TABLESPOON RICE VINEGAR
- 1 TABLESPOON RED CURRY PASTE
- 2 TEASPOONS THAI OR VIETNAMESE FISH SAUCE
- 1 SMALL SWEET ONION, SUCH AS MAUI, ABOUT 3 OUNCES, DICED FINE
- ¼ BUNCH FRESH CILANTRO, LEAVES AND STEMS CHOPPED FINE
- 15 TO 20 FRESH THAI OR EUROPEAN BASIL LEAVES (USE FEWER THAI LEAVES), CHOPPED FINE
- 1 KAFFIR LIME LEAF, CHOPPED FINE, OR 1 TEASPOON GRATED LIME ZEST
- 1 TEASPOON MINCED GARLIC
- 1 TEASPOON MINCED GINGERROOT
- 4 TABLESPOONS UNSALTED BUTTER, CUT INTO BITS

Combine all the ingredients except the butter in a saucepan and bring to a simmer over medium heat. Lower the heat and cook, uncovered, at a bare simmer until the coconut oil rises to the surface, about an hour. If sauce thickens and begins to stick, thin it with a little hot water. When there is a film of coconut oil completely covering the sauce, remove it from the heat and stir well. Reserve until you're ready to cook the fish.

When ready to cook the fish, heat ½ cup of the peanut sauce over low heat. Whisk in the butter, a few bits at a time, and remove from the heat.

SWORDFISH

- 1¾ POUNDS SWORDFISH, SKINNED AND CUT INTO EVEN PORTIONS ABOUT ½ INCH THICK
- SALT
- 2 TABLESPOONS LEMONGRASS, MINCED FINE
- 1 TABLESPOON MINCED GARLIC
- 1 TABLESPOON MINCED SHALLOTS
- 1 TABLESPOON MINCED GINGERROOT
- 1 TEASPOON HICHIMI (JAPANESE SEVEN-PEPPER SPICE)
- 2 TABLESPOONS CANOLA OR VEGETABLE OIL
- OPTIONAL GARNISH: RADISH SPROUTS AND RED PICKLED GINGER

Season the fish lightly with salt. Combine lemongrass, garlic, shallots, gingerroot, and hichimi in a small bowl. Spread the mixture on one side of the swordfish and let stand about 5 minutes.

Drizzle the coated side of the fish with the oil. Heat a nonstick sauté pan over medium-high heat. When the pan is hot, add the fish, coated side down. Cook 1 to 1½ minutes, until the edges are just opaque. Turn the swordfish and cook an additional 1 to 1½ minutes.

Place the fish, crusted side up, on serving plates. Pour the sauce around the fish. Garnish the top of the fish with radish sprouts and red pickled ginger, if desired.

Annie Roberts's Grilled Leg of Lamb with Wine Vinaigrette

SERVES 6 TO 8

In this recipe, Annie plays on lamb's affinity with wine, herbs, and acid ingredients. She has designed the dish so the lamb and vinaigrette can be marinated and prepared a day ahead, making the cook's work only grilling on the day of service. If you use rosemary in the marinade, use parsley in the vinaigrette.

Marinade and Lamb

- **3 garlic cloves, chopped**
- **2 tablespoons chopped fresh rosemary or basil leaves**
- **1 tablespoon crushed black pepper**
- **¼ cup olive oil**
- **1 leg of lamb, 5 to 6 pounds, boned and butterflied**

Mix together the garlic, rosemary or basil, black pepper, and oil. Place the lamb in a dish that holds it comfortably and spread the marinade all over the lamb. Cover and refrigerate for at least 4 hours, or preferably overnight, turning the lamb two or three times.

Vinaigrette

- **¼ cup Cabernet Sauvignon**
- **¼ cup red wine vinegar**
- **2 shallots, diced fine**
- **1 cup seeded and diced tomato**
- **¼ cup chopped fresh basil or Italian parsley leaves**
- **1 garlic clove, chopped**
- **½ cup olive oil**
- **Salt and fresh-ground pepper to taste**

Combine the wine and vinegar in a small nonreactive saucepan with the shallots. Cook over high heat until 2 tablespoons of liquid remain.

Combine the tomato, basil or parsley, and garlic in a food processor and add the reduced wine mixture. With the motor running, pour in the olive oil in a fine stream until the vinaigrette emulsifies. Season with salt and pepper. If you make the vinaigrette the day before, cover and refrigerate it. Remove it from the refrigerator about 1½ hours before serving.

To Finish the Lamb

Remove the lamb from the refrigerator 1½ hours before you're ready to cook it. Prepare a medium-hot grill, preferably of mesquite charcoal.

When ready to cook, place the skin side of the lamb toward the coals. Check to be sure the lamb is not cooking too quickly. Turn the lamb as necessary and grill until it is rare, 15 to 25 minutes.

Remove the lamb from the grill and let it rest 10 minutes before slicing it about ¼ inch thick on a diagonal. Place the sliced lamb on a serving platter and pour over any juices from slicing. Nap the lamb with some of the vinaigrette and pass the remainder.

Seasons of the Vineyard
212

FUMÉ BLANC LEMON-DILL VINAIGRETTE

Plan to make this lovely-tasting vinaigrette when you are serving a large group of people, the more to share it with, and because it is best used within a day or two of making. Sarah Scott discovered another fine use for Fumé Blanc when she created this recipe. The vinaigrette is excellent on cold vegetables, particularly asparagus, cauliflower, and carrots; it also makes a wonderful potato salad, and avocado vinaigrette.

 1 BOTTLE (750 ML) FUMÉ BLANC

 3 SHALLOTS, DICED FINE

 GRATED ZEST AND JUICE OF 1 LEMON

1½ TABLESPOONS RICE VINEGAR

 ABOUT 1¼ CUPS OLIVE OIL

½ BUNCH FRESH DILL, LEAVES CHOPPED FINE

 SALT AND FRESH-GROUND PEPPER

Reduce the Fumé Blanc in a nonreactive saucepan to about ¾ cup. Place the diced shallots in a medium-size bowl and pour the hot wine over them. Steep the shallots for at least 15 minutes.

Chop the lemon zest fine and add it to the shallots. Add the lemon juice and the rice vinegar and mix well.

Whisk in the olive oil in a fine stream to make an emulsion. Taste as you add the oil, until the flavor is balanced as you like it. Stir in the chopped dill and season the vinaigrette with salt and pepper. Keep refrigerated until ready to use.

GREEN BEANS WITH MINT

This is a special dish when the first green beans come in, about ¼ inch in diameter and 3 to 6 inches long. Helen Mondavi Ventura, who contributed this recipe of her mother, Rosa, prefers the beans without any vinegar or lemon juice, but says some in the family like the beans dressed with a little.

 3 POUNDS TENDER GREEN BEANS

 3 TABLESPOONS EXTRA-VIRGIN OLIVE OIL

 4 LARGE GARLIC CLOVES, MINCED

 8 TO 10 LARGE FRESH MINT SPRIGS, LEAVES
    CHOPPED

 SALT AND FRESH-GROUND PEPPER

 OPTIONAL: WHITE WINE VINEGAR OR LEMON JUICE

Top and tail the beans if they are large and/or tough when snapped raw. When the beans are young, it will not be necessary. Rinse the beans and blanch them in boiling water until they are just crisp-tender and a bright green, about 5 minutes for tender beans.

Drain the beans and refresh them under cold water; drain again.

Add the olive oil and garlic to a sauté pan large enough to hold the beans comfortably. Place over medium heat and cook until the garlic gives an aroma, about a minute. Add the beans and reduce the heat to low. Add the mint and cook for 3 or 4 minutes. Remove from the heat and season well with salt and pepper.

Serve the beans warm or at room temperature. Sprinkle with a little white wine vinegar or lemon juice, if desired.

Bread Salad
with Fennel and Red Pepper

Good bread is such a treat that it is a shame to throw it out or feed it to the birds. Annie Roberts, inspired by the Tuscan bread salad, *panzanella*, devised this simple, very tasty salad to use leftover bread. It can be served as a first course, or alongside roast chicken, or accompany anything from the grill. Full-flavored wine, white or red, will go happily with it.

8 OUNCES DAY- OR TWO-DAY-OLD SOURDOUGH OR COUNTRY-STYLE BREAD

ABOUT ⅓ CUP EXTRA-VIRGIN OLIVE OIL

1 FRESH FENNEL BULB, ABOUT 1 POUND

1 LARGE RED BELL PEPPER, ROASTED, PEELED, AND DEVEINED (PAGE 133)

1 RED ONION, HALVED LENGTHWISE AND SLICED THIN

24 KALAMATA OLIVES, PITTED AND CHOPPED COARSE

½ CUP CHOPPED FRESH BASIL LEAVES

¼ CUP RED WINE VINEGAR

SALT AND FRESH-GROUND PEPPER

Preheat the oven to 300° F. Cut the bread in 1-inch cubes. Toss with 2 tablespoons of the olive oil, then spread on a baking sheet and bake until crisp, about 15 minutes. Cool to room temperature.

Trim the fennel bulb and cut in half lengthwise. Slice thin crosswise. Cut the bell pepper in about ¼-inch strips.

Combine the bread, fennel, bell pepper, onion, olives, and basil in a serving dish. Whisk the vinegar together with the remaining olive oil in a small bowl. Season the vinaigrette lightly with salt and pepper.

Toss the salad with the vinaigrette. Let the salad stand for 20 minutes or so to marry the flavors. Adjust the seasoning with vinegar, oil, salt, or pepper, if necessary. Serve at cool room temperature.

ROSA MONDAVI'S TOMATO CONSERVA

The cook whose pantry contains some jars of this tomato sauce will have some options for summery-tasting dishes in other seasons. Use the conserva anywhere tomato sauce is an important element of the dish—with pasta, pizza, soups, and stews. A food mill is necessary for this recipe; it handily strains the tomato seeds and skins and gives a lovely texture to the sauce. It is handy to pack the conserva in both pints and half-pints; once the jars are opened they should be stored in the refrigerator, for up to 5 days.

9 POUNDS RIPE PLUM TOMATOES

3 CARROTS, PEELED

3 ONIONS

2 CELERY STALKS

ABOUT 2 TABLESPOON SALT, OR TO TASTE

7 OR 8 LARGE FRESH BASIL SPRIGS

7 OR 8 LARGE FRESH ITALIAN PARSLEY SPRIGS

Core the tomatoes, halve them, and place them in a large nonreactive pot. Chop the carrots, onions, and celery and add them to the tomatoes. Add 2 teaspoons salt to the vegetables.

Cover the pot and place it over high heat. When the tomatoes begin to give up their juices, lower the heat and cook the vegetables at a bare simmer for about an hour. Tie the basil and parsley sprigs together with kitchen string and add them to the vegetables. Cook, uncovered, for another hour, or until the vegetables are very soft and the sauce is thick.

Meanwhile, sterilize canning jars and lids. Bring a kettle of water to boil.

Remove the basil and parsley from the sauce and adjust the salt. Press the sauce in batches through a food mill into a bowl. Ladle the hot sauce into the hot canning jars and cover them with lids and rings according to manufacturer's directions.

Place the jars in the kettle and water-bath the conserva for 10 minutes. Remove the jars with canning tongs and cool to room temperature. Refrigerate any jars that do not seal, and use them within a week. Keep jars that did seal in a cool, dark place for up to a year.

Michael Chipchase's Lemon Curd Tart with Summer Berries

Here Vineyard Room chef Michael Chipchase features the abundant berries of summer next to a light-tasting but rich lemon curd. The contrast between the various textures and flavors of the berries and the luscious, smooth curd is refreshing, particularly after a simple alfresco meal from the grill. The tart is especially enjoyable with a glass of slightly chilled dessert wine from Muscat Canelli or botrytised white wine grapes.

The pastry dough that is used throughout this book may be fitted into tart pans and frozen for up to two weeks ahead. Bake it without thawing. As the dough is rather short, place the tart pan on a baking sheet before it goes into the oven. You will need only one portion of the dough for the tart; freeze the remaining portion for another pie or tart.

TART

PASTRY DOUGH (PAGE 193)

6 **LARGE EGG YOLKS, LIGHTLY BEATEN**

1 **CUP SUGAR**

½ **CUP LEMON JUICE (2 OR 3 LEMONS)**

8 **TABLESPOONS UNSALTED BUTTER, CUT INTO SMALL CUBES**

1 **TABLESPOON GRATED LEMON ZEST**

Divide the dough in half and roll one portion to fit a 9-inch tart pan with removable bottom; reserve the other portion for another use. Place the pan in the freezer while you prepare the filling. Preheat the oven to 400° F.

Combine the egg yolks in a heavy-bottomed saucepan with the sugar and lemon juice. Cook over medium-low heat, stirring continually, for 10 to 15 minutes, until the mixture has thickened. Remove from the heat and whisk in the butter, a few pieces at a time, and the lemon zest.

When the dough has rested for at least 15 minutes, line the shell with aluminum foil and beans or pie weights. Bake for 15 minutes. Remove the foil and weights and reduce the heat to 375° F. Bake the crust until it is a rich golden brown, 10 to 15 minutes. Remove to a rack to cool.

Pour the cooled curd into the cooled tart shell and refrigerate at least 30 minutes before slicing.

BERRIES

1 **PINT STRAWBERRIES**

½ **PINT RASPBERRIES**

½ **PINT BLUEBERRIES**

1 **TABLESPOON GRAND MARNIER OR COINTREAU**

CONFECTIONERS' SUGAR

GARNISH: 8 SMALL FRESH MINT SPRIGS

Sort and rinse the berries and drain them well. Just before serving, mix them in a bowl with the Grand Marnier. Sprinkle with a little confectioners' sugar if the berries need sweetening. Cut the tart into wedges and divide among serving plates. Spoon the berries next to the tart and garnish with mint sprigs.

Marcella Hazan's Lemon Ice Cream

MAKES ABOUT 1 PINT

Marcella writes of her luscious, lemony ice cream, "Aroma is the clue to successful lemon ice cream. Here it is extracted from the rind, which is boiled with water and sugar to make a syrup." For a relatively low-fat ice cream like this, you will need an ice-cream maker that works quickly. The ice cream may be still-frozen by completely breaking it up and mixing every 2 or 3 hours; the texture will not be as smooth as that made in a machine, though the ice cream will still be delicious.

1 ½ CUPS WATER
  ½ CUP TIGHTLY PACKED LEMON PEEL (OUTER
     YELLOW SKIN WITH NONE OF THE WHITE PITH
     BENEATH), FROM 4 TO 6 LEMONS
   1 CUP SUGAR
  ⅔ CUP FRESHLY SQUEEZED LEMON JUICE
  ⅔ CUP WHIPPING CREAM

Place the water, lemon peel, sugar, and lemon juice in a nonreactive saucepan and bring to a boil. Boil for 2 minutes, then strain the syrup into a bowl. Cool to room temperature, then chill thoroughly.

When ready to freeze the ice cream, stir in the whipping cream, then pour into an ice cream maker and freeze according to manufacturer's instructions.

Moscato d'Oro Sorbet

MAKES ABOUT 1 ½ PINTS

Rather than a glass of Moscato d'Oro, try a little of this sorbet as a refreshing end to a summer meal. Fresh berries, peaches, or nectarines are natural accompaniments. Because the sorbet is practically pure wine, you will need an ice cream maker with some power to freeze it. For a granita-like texture, the sorbet may be still-frozen a day ahead and broken up three or four times with a fork.

   1 BOTTLE (750 ML) MOSCATO D'ORO
  ⅓ CUP SUGAR

Measure ⅔ cup of wine and refrigerate the remaining wine. Place the measured wine and the sugar in a nonreactive saucepan. Heat over medium heat, stirring frequently, until the sugar has dissolved. Cool the mixture to room temperature.

Mix the wine and sugar with the refrigerated wine and chill thoroughly. Pour the mixture into an ice cream maker and freeze according to manufacturer's directions. Or, pour the mixture into a 8- or 9-inch nonreactive metal baking pan and place in the freezer. Freeze for 24 hours, breaking and distributing the ice crystals three or four times.

Serve the sorbet in chilled dishes.

To Your Health

Liquid and Dry Measure Equivalencies

Customary		Metric
¼	teaspoon	1.25 milliliters
½	teaspoon	2.5 milliliters
1	teaspoon	5 milliliters
1	tablespoon	15 milliliters
1	fluid ounce	30 milliliters
¼	cup	60 milliliters
⅓	cup	80 milliliters
½	cup	120 milliliters
1	cup	240 milliliters
1	pint (2 cups)	480 milliliters
1	quart (4 cups; 32 ounces)	960 milliliters (.96 liter)
1	gallon (4 quarts)	3.84 liters
1	ounce (by weight)	28 grams
¼	pound (4 ounces)	114 grams
1	pound (16 opunces)	454 grams
2.2	pounds	1 kilogram (1,000 grams)

Oven Temperature Equivalents

Description	Fahrenheit	Celsius
Cool	200	90
Very slow	250	120
Slow	300–325	150–160
Moderately slow	325–350	160–180
Moderate	350–375	180–190
Moderately hot	375–400	190–200
Hot	400–450	200–230
Very hot	450–500	230–260

Index